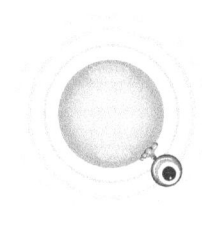

Answer Book

Whole Number

Fractions, Decimals and Percentages

Algebraic Thinking

Contents

Whole Number Pupil Book 1

Whole Number PPMs

Whole Number APMs

Fractions, Decimals and Percentages Pupil Book 2

Fractions, Decimals and Percentages PPMs

Fractions, Decimals and Percentages APMs

Algebraic Thinking Pupil Book 3

Algebraic Thinking PPMs

Algebraic Thinking APMs

Whole Number Pupil Book 1

Page 3
6-digit numbers

1. a: 576 400
   b: 576 100
   c: 576 200
   d: 576 300
   e: 576 700
   f: 576 000
   g: 576 800
   h: 576 900
   i: 577 000
2. 56 402 > 29 617
3. 64 782 < 730 212
4. 300 803 > 54 660
5. 278 920 > 12 786
6. 104 202 > 99 999
7. 37 472 < 827 406

Rocket 101 numbers (10 999 to 11 099 inclusive)

Page 4
6-digit numbers

1. 59 473, 60 473, 61 473, 62 473
2. 24 908, 25 008, 25 108, 25 208
3. 36 419, 26 419, 16 419, 6419
4. 192 308, 202 308, 212 308, 222 308
5. 905 606, 1 005 606, 1 105 606, 1 205 606
6. 75 939, 75 949, 75 959, 75 969
7. 785 620, 784 620, 783 620, 782 620
8. 64 547, 64 647, 64 747, 64 847
9. 464 940, 364 940, 264 940, 164 940
10. 542 624, 552 624, 562 624, 572 624
11. False
12. False
13. True
14. True

Rocket 999 999 (1 000 001 to 1 999 999 inclusive)

Page 5
Negative numbers

1. −3
2. −2
3. −6
4. −3
5. 4
6. −1
7. 5
8. 2
9. −1
10. 6
11. Answers will vary.

Rocket 70 days to get to 0°C if it rises by $\frac{1}{2}$°C each day; 140 days if it rises by $\frac{1}{4}$°C each day; 46.66 days if it rises by $\frac{3}{4}$°C each day.

Page 6
Negative numbers

1. −5°C
2. −1°C
3. −9°C
4. −4°C
5. 3°C
6. −4°C
7. Paris: −3°C
   Copenhagen: −4°C
   London: 3°C
   Madrid: 9°C
   Berlin: −6°C
   Rome: 7°C
   Moscow: −11°C
   Warsaw: −9°C
   Prague: −8°C

Rocket Answers will vary.

Page 7
Divisibility

1. No
2. Yes
3. Yes
4. Yes
5. No
6. Yes
7. No
8. No
9. Yes
10. No
11. Yes
12. Yes
13. No
14. Yes
15. Yes

Rocket Numbers of pairs:
2. 28 pairs
3. 42 pairs
4. 69 pairs
6. 27 pairs
9. 193 pairs
11. 504 pairs
12. 239 pairs
14. 82 pairs
15. 150 pairs

Can be grouped in fours:
2. Yes
3. Yes
4. No
6. No
9. No
11. Yes
12. No
14. Yes
15. Yes

16. Answers will vary. For example: 6, 10, 14.
17. Answers will vary. For example: 5, 15, 25.
18. Answers will vary. For example: 5, 15, 25.
19. Answers will vary. For example: 4, 8, 12.
20. Answers will vary. For example: 7, 11, 13.

Rocket 50 numbers divisible by 2; 25 numbers divisible by 4; 20 numbers divisible by 5; 5 numbers divisible by 2, 4 and 5.

Page 8
Tests of divisibility

1.

	2	3	4	5	6	8	9	10	25	50
140	✓		✓	✓				✓		
270	✓	✓		✓	✓		✓	✓		
3000	✓	✓	✓	✓	✓	✓		✓	✓	✓
85				✓						
76	✓		✓							
432	✓	✓	✓		✓	✓	✓			
175				✓					✓	
234	✓	✓			✓		✓			
875				✓					✓	
4134	✓	✓			✓					

2. Answers will vary. For example, 189 000 has ten ticks.

Rocket Answers will vary. There is no divisibility test for 7.

Page 9
Multiplying by 100 and 1000

1. 36 100
   Value = 30 thousand
2. 45 200
   Value = 5 thousand
3. 6800
   Value = 8 hundred
4. 71 600
   Value = 1 thousand
5. 60 500
   Value = 60 thousand
6. 42 400
   Value = 40 thousand
7. 28 100
   Value = 1 hundred
8. 34 800
   Value = 30 thousand
9. 11 000
   Value = 1 thousand
10. 19 300
    Value = 9 thousand
11. 9100
    Value = 1 hundred
12. 76 300
    Value = 6 thousand

Rocket Six times

13. 4300
14. 760 200
15. 351 000
16. 8 080 000
17. 5 010 000
18. 764 000

Page 10
Calculating with 10, 100 and 1000

1. a and d   b and t
   f and o   g and s
   k and c   l and n
   p and w   q and x
   u and y   v and i

2. 1200 months in a century, 12 000 months in a millennium, 5200 weeks in a century, 52 000 weeks in a millennium.
3. £47 to drive 100 miles, £470 to drive 1000 miles.
4. £1500 after 100 weeks, £1560 after 2 years.
5. 273 × 100 = 27 300
6. 3600 ÷ 10 = 360
7. 4875 × 10 = 48 750
8. 3 140 000 ÷ 1000 = 3140
9. 402 × 1000 = 402 000
10. 76 × 1000 = 76 000
11. 5138 × 100 = 513 800
12. 620 × 10 = 6200
13. 53 000 ÷ 100 = 530

Rocket Answers may vary. It should take the person multiplying by 10 six times to reach over a million, and the person multiplying by 100 three times. However, the number of times it takes you to reach over six million depends upon your start number.

Page 11
2s, 3s, 4s, 5s, 10s

1. 12, 14, 16, 18
2. 18, 21, 24, 27
3. 20, 24, 28, 32
4. 30, 35, 40, 45
5. 50, 60, 70, 80

Rocket 24 multiples of 2 under 50; 16 multiples of 3 under 50; 12 multiples of 4 under 50; 9 multiples of 5 under 50.

6. Multiples of 5: 35, 40, 45, 50, 55, 60, 65, 70; Multiples of 10: 40, 50, 60, 70; Numbers in both lists: 40, 50, 60, 70.
7. Multiples of 2: 2, 4, 6, 8, 10, 12, 14, 16, 18, 20, 22, 24, 26, 28, 30; Multiples of 3: 3, 6, 9, 12, 15, 18, 21, 24, 27, 30; Numbers in both lists: 6, 12, 18, 24, 30.

Page 12
Multiples

1. True
2. False
3. True
4. False
5. True
6. True
7. 16 → 1 point; 21 → 3 points; total 4 points
8. 25 → 2 points; 9 → 3 points; 14 → 1 point; total 6 points
9. total 0 points
10. 26 → 1 point; 35 → 2 points; 21 → 3 points; total 6 points
11. 27 → 3 points; 4 → 1 point; 3 → 3 points; total 7 points
12. 35 → 2 points; 8 → 1 point; 28 → 1 point; total 4 points
13. 10
14. 6
15. 25
16. 100
17. 20
18. 50

Page 13
Common multiples

1. 7, 14, 21, 28, 35, 42, 49, 56, 63, 70
2. 4, 8, 12, 16, 20, 24, 28, 32, 36, 40, 48, 56, 60, 64, 72, 80, 100
3. 9, 18, 27, 36, 45, 54, 63, 72, 81, 90
4. 6, 12, 18, 24, 30, 36, 42, 48, 54, 60, 72, 90
5. 12, 24, 36, 48, 60, 72
6. 14, 28, 42, 56, 70
7. 12, 24, 36, 48, 60, 72
8. 8, 16, 24, 32, 40, 48, 56, 64, 72, 80
9. 20, 40, 60, 80, 100

Rocket Answers can vary. Possible answers include: 60 (a common multiple of 3, 4 and 5; also of 4, 5 and 6); 6 (a common multiple of 1, 2 and 3); 210 (a common multiple of 5, 6 and 7).

10. 6
11. 10
12. 12
13. 15
14. 4
15. 12
16. 12
17. 24
18. 24
19. 40
20. 30
21. 150

Page 14
Factors

1. 20 → 1 × 20, 2 × 10, 4 × 5
2. 18 → 1 × 18, 2 × 9, 3 × 6
3. 30 → 1 × 30, 2 × 15, 3 × 10, 5 × 6
4. 14 → 1 × 14, 2 × 7
5. 40 → 1 × 40, 2 × 20, 4 × 10, 5 × 8
6. 32 → 1 × 32, 2 × 16, 4 × 8
7. 54 → 1 × 54, 2 × 27, 3 × 18, 6 × 9
8. 63 → 1 × 63, 3 × 21, 7 × 9

Lists of factors:
1. 20: 1, 2, 4, 5, 10, 20
2. 18: 1, 2, 3, 6, 9, 18
3. 30: 1, 2, 3, 5, 6, 10, 15, 30
4. 14: 1, 2, 7, 14
5. 40: 1, 2, 4, 5, 8, 10, 20, 40
6. 32: 1, 2, 4, 8, 16, 32
7. 54: 1, 2, 3, 6, 9, 18, 27, 54
8. 63: 1, 3, 7, 9, 21, 63

Rocket Answers will vary. For example, 42 has 1 and 42, 2 and 21, 3 and 14, 6 and 7.

9. 6: 1, 2, 3, 6
10. 16: 1, 2, 4, 8, 16
11. 10: 1, 2, 5, 10
12. 50: 1, 2, 5, 10, 25, 50
13. 28: 1, 2, 4, 7, 14, 28
14. 48: 1, 2, 3, 4, 6, 8, 12, 16, 24, 48
15. 60: 1, 2, 3, 4, 5, 6, 10, 12, 15, 20, 30, 60
16. 52: 1, 2, 4, 13, 26, 52
17. 3
18. 4
19. 9
20. 7 or 28
21. 1
22. 5

Page 15
Prime numbers

Rocket Answers will vary but could include: 101, 103, 107, 109, 113, 127.

1. False
2. True
3. True
4. False
5. False
6. True
7. True
8. False
9. True
10. True
11. True
12. True

Rocket 17 and 73; 19 and 71; 23 and 67; 29 and 61; 31 and 59; 37 and 53; 43 and 47

Page 16
Re-ordering numbers

1. 120
2. 210
3. 180
4. 240
5. 72
6. 2500
7. 120
8. 84
9. 270
10. 648
11. 756
12. 2016

Rocket Answers will vary.

Page 17
Using brackets

1. £29
2. £35
3. £25
4. £23
5. £31
6. £30
7. £28
8. £26

Rocket Answers will vary.

9. 32
10. 38
11. 29
12. 28
13. 31
14. 24
15. 29
16. 28

Page 18
Using brackets

1. £220
2. £310
3. £280
4. £230
5. £260
6. £290
7. £180
8. Bogwash: 340 cm
   Treacleflower: 380 cm
   Googlygorse: 280 cm
   Squiffleweed: 330 cm
   Bumbleroot: 340 cm
   Bogglerot: 340 cm

9. January: 340 cm; February: 370 cm; March: 370 cm; April: 360 cm; May: 310 cm; June: 260 cm

Rocket Bogwash: 460 cm
Treacleflower: 500 cm
Googlygorse: 400 cm
Squiffleweed: 450 cm
Bumbleroot: 460 cm
Bogglerot: 460 cm

Page 19
Using brackets

1. £19, £1 change
2. £18, £2 change
3. £16, £4 change
4. £18, £2 change

Rocket £1

5. 2100
6. 2000
7. 2500
8. 1500
9. 1700
10. 1800

Page 20
Using brackets and partitioning

1. $3 \times 43 = (3 \times 40) + (3 \times 3)$
   $= 120 + 9 = 129$
2. $4 \times 36 = (4 \times 30) + (4 \times 6)$
   $= 120 + 24 = 144$
3. $5 \times 27 = (5 \times 20) + (5 \times 7)$
   $= 100 + 35 = 135$
4. $9 \times 17 = (9 \times 10) + (9 \times 7)$
   $= 90 + 63 = 153$
5. $7 \times 52 = (7 \times 50) + (7 \times 2)$
   $= 350 + 14 = 364$
6. $6 \times 24 = (6 \times 20) + (6 \times 4)$
   $= 120 + 24 = 144$
7. $8 \times 32 = (8 \times 30) + (8 \times 2)$
   $= 240 + 16 = 256$
8. 32 p
   × 3
   ―――
   90   3 × 30
   6   3 × 2
   ―――
   96 p

9. 28 p
   × 4
   ―――
   80   4 × 20
   32   4 × 8
   ―――
   112p or £1·12

10. 42 p
    × 5
    ―――
    200   5 × 40
    10   5 × 2
    ―――
    210p or £2·10

11. 46 p
    × 7
    ―――
    280   7 × 40
    42   7 × 6
    ―――
    322p or £3·22

12. 28 p
    × 3
    ―――
    60   3 × 20
    24   3 × 8
    ―――
    84 p

    32 p
    × 4
    ―――
    120   4 × 30
    8   4 × 2
    ―――
    128p or £1·28

    84p + £1·28 = £2·12

Rocket Answers will vary. Lowest possible cost: $4 \times 28p = £1·12$; highest possible cost: $4 \times 46p = £1·84$.

Page 21
Using brackets and partitioning

1. $(6 \times 50) + (6 \times 6)$
   $300 + 36 = 336$
2. $(8 \times 30) + (8 \times 7)$
   $240 + 56 = 296$
3. $(5 \times 70) + (5 \times 8)$
   $350 + 40 = 390$
4. $(7 \times 40) + (7 \times 7)$
   $280 + 49 = 329$
5. $(6 \times 60) + (6 \times 4)$
   $360 + 24 = 384$
6. $(7 \times 20) + (7 \times 9)$
   $140 + 63 = 203$
7. $(5 \times 20) + (5 \times 3)$
   $100 + 15 = 115$
8. $(3 \times 30) + (3 \times 2)$
   $90 + 6 = 96$
9. $(8 \times 30) + (8 \times 4)$
   $240 + 32 = 272$
10. $(6 \times 60) + (6 \times 8)$
    $360 + 48 = £408$
11. $(8 \times 70) + (8 \times 2)$
    $560 + 16 = £576$
12. $(7 \times 40) + (7 \times 4)$
    $280 + 28 = £308$
13. $(7 \times 30) + (7 \times 6)$
    $210 + 42 = £252$
14. $(8 \times 60) + (8 \times 4)$
    $480 + 32 = £512$
15. $(6 \times 50) + (6 \times 9)$
    $300 + 54 = £354$
16. $(6 \times 20) + (6 \times 2)$
    $120 + 12 = £132$
17. $(8 \times 80) + (8 \times 7)$
    $640 + 56 = £696$
18. $(7 \times 100) + (7 \times 40) + (7 \times 5)$
    $700 + 280 + 35 = £1015$

Rocket Methods may vary but may include adding together the ×20 and ×1 tables, or the ×10 and ×11 tables.

$21 \times 1 = 21$
$21 \times 2 = 42$
$21 \times 3 = 63$
$21 \times 4 = 84$
$21 \times 5 = 105$
$21 \times 6 = 126$
$21 \times 7 = 147$
$21 \times 8 = 168$
$21 \times 9 = 189$
$21 \times 10 = 210$

Page 22
Using brackets and partitioning

1. Estimate 300; $3 \times 146 = (3 \times 100) + (3 \times 40) + (3 \times 6) = 300 + 120 + 18 = 438$
2. Estimate 1000; $5 \times 243 = (5 \times 200) + (5 \times 40) + (5 \times 3) = 1000 + 200 + 15 = 1215$
3. Estimate 1200; $4 \times 317 = (4 \times 300) + (4 \times 10) + (4 \times 7) = 1200 + 40 + 28 = 1268$
4. Estimate 600; $6 \times 128 = (6 \times 100) + (6 \times 20) + (6 \times 8) = 600 + 120 + 48 = 768$
5. $3 \times 416 = (3 \times 400) + (3 \times 10) + (3 \times 6) = 1200 + 30 + 18 = 1248$
6. $279 \times 5 = (5 \times 200) + (5 \times 70) + (5 \times 9) = 1000 + 350 + 45 = 1395$
7. $186 \times 7 = (7 \times 100) + (7 \times 80) + (7 \times 6) = 700 + 560 + 42 = 1302$
8. $304 \times 6 = (6 \times 300) + (6 \times 4) = 1800 + 24 = 1824$
9. $512 \times 4 = (4 \times 500) + (4 \times 10) + (4 \times 2) = 2000 + 40 + 8 = 2048$
10. $484 \times 3 = (3 \times 400) + (3 \times 80) + (3 \times 4) = 1200 + 240 + 12 = 1452$
11. £1644
12. £561
13. £1472
14. £1008
15. £3038
16. £4175

Rocket
11. 7
12. 10
13. 5
14. 15
15. 4
16. 2

Page 23
Using partitioning

1. 810
2. 490
3. 210
4. 990
5. 400
6. 840
7. 330
8. 672
9. 544
10. 330
11. 450
12. 399
13. 368
14. 425
15. 432

Rocket Answers will vary but may include 40×12, 48×10, 60×8, 120×4.

Page 24
Using brackets and partitioning

10	20	30	40	50	60	70	80	90	100
2	4	6	8	10	12	14	16	18	20
12	24	36	48	60	72	84	96	108	120

1. $(12 \times 20) + (12 \times 3)$
   $240 + 36 = 276$

2. (12 × 20) + (12 × 7)
   240 + 84 = 324
3. (12 × 30) + (12 × 1)
   360 + 12 = 372
4. (12 × 40) + (12 × 3)
   480 + 36 = 516
5. (12 × 30) + (12 × 5)
   360 + 60 = 420
6. (12 × 40) + (12 × 7)
   480 + 84 = 564
7. (12 × 50) + (12 × 2)
   600 + 24 = 624
8. (12 × 40) + (12 × 2)
   480 + 24 = 504
9. (12 × 30) + (12 × 9)
   360 + 108 = 468
10. (12 × 40) + (12 × 8)
    480 + 96 = 576
11. (12 × 30) + (12 × 3)
    360 + 36 = 396
12. (12 × 20) + (12 × 8)
    240 + 96 = 336

Rocket

10	20	30	40	50	60	70	80	90	100
3	6	9	12	15	18	21	24	27	30
13	26	39	52	65	78	91	104	117	130

Other answers will vary.

Page 25
Order of operations

1. 12 + 3 − 6 = 9
2. 45 − 7 + 37 = 75
3. 350 + 250 − 175 = 425
4. 48 + 92 − 39 = 101
5. 625 − 50 + 75 = 650
6. 175 + 225 − 80 = 320

Rocket Answers will vary.

7. (2 × 10) + (4 × 6)
   20 + 24 = 44
8. (4 ÷ 2) + (6 × 1)
   2 + 6 = 8
9. 6 + (4 × 3) + 1
   6 + 12 + 1 = 19
10. 7 − (3 ÷ 1) + 2
    7 − 3 + 2 = 6
11. 3 + (4 ÷ 2) + 5
    3 + 2 + 5 = 10
12. 60 + (40 ÷ 10) + 20
    60 + 4 + 20 = 84

Page 26
Rounding

1. 5983 → 6000
2. 3812 → 3800
3. 3501 → 3500
4. 8712 → 8700
5. 6574 → 6600
6. 4329 → 4300
7. 2863 → 2900
8. 7750 → 7800
9. £468 → £500
10. £3750 → £3800
11. £16 458 → £16 500
12. £271 → £300
13. £28 650 → £28 700
14. £5127 → £5100
15. £6833 → £6800
16. £724 → £700
17. £80
18. Answers will vary.

Rocket Answers will vary.

Page 27
Rounding

1. 4328 →   a: 4300   b: 4330
2. 6795 →   a: 6800   b: 6800
3. 3827 →   a: 3800   b: 3830
4. 13 452 →   a: 13 500   b: 13 450
5. 11 261 →   a: 11 300   b: 11 260
6. 8875 →   a: 8900   b: 8880
7. 6983 →   a: 7000   b: 6980
8. 8914 →   a: 8900   b: 8910
9. 9276 →   a: 9300   b: 9280
10. 15 589 → 15 600
11. 12 741 → 12 700
12. 18 151 → 18 200
13. 20 247 → 20 200
14. 15 858 → 15 900
15. 13 604 → 13 600

Rocket
10. 4300 + 11 300 = 15 600
11. 8900 + 3800 = 12 700
12. 9300 + 8900 = 18 200
13. 6800 + 13 500 = 20 300
14. 7000 + 8900 = 15 900
15. 4300 + 9300 = 13 600

You get a different answer than if you added first, then rounded.

Page 28
Rounding

1. a: 6560 → 7000
   b: 6360 → 6000
   c: 6910 → 7000
   d: 6170 → 6000
   e: 6730 → 7000
2. f: 5311 → 5300
   g: 5347 → 5300
   h: 5372 → 5400
   i: 5334 → 5300
   j: 5388 → 5400
3. k: 2752 → 2750
   l: 2789 → 2790
   m: 2719 → 2720
   n: 2774 → 2770
   p: 2737 → 2740
4. a: £8146 → £8000
   b: £8100
   c: £8150
5. a: £7234 → £7000
   b: £7200
   c: £7230
6. a: £3974 → £4000
   b: £4000
   c: £3980
7. a: £9148 → £9000
   b: £9100
   c: £9150
8. a: £5158 → £5000
   b: £5200
   c: £5160
9. a: £11 762 → £12 000
   b: £11 800
   c: £11 760
10. a: £12 349 → £12 000
    b: £12 300
    c: £12 350
11. a: £6695 → £7000
    b: £6700
    c: £6700
12. a: £15 685 → £16 000
    b: £15 700
    c: £15 690

Rocket Answers will vary but include any 4-digit numbers ending in the range 995–004, for example 1995 or 5002.

Page 29
Rounding

1. 27 564 →   a: 28 000   b: 27 600
2. 18 546 →   a: 19 000   b: 18 500
3. 43 582 →   a: 44 000   b: 43 600
4. 13 712 →   a: 14 000   b: 13 700
5. 64 789 →   a: 65 000   b: 64 800
6. 34 358 →   a: 34 000   b: 34 400

Rocket Answers will vary.

7. Total number of spectators: 10 499 → 10 500; Money made on programmes: £31 497
8. £14 000
9. a: 3650   b: 3749
10. a: 74 500   b: 75 499
11. a: 4855   b: 4864
12. a: 468 500 b: 469 499
13. a: 58 650   b: 58 749
14. a: 47 385   b: 47 394

Page 30
Working backwards and forwards

1.   9 6 7
    + 1 5 4
    ─────────
    1 1 2 1
       1 1

2.   4 2 4 6
    + 9 2 8 3
    ─────────
    1 3 5 2 9
           1

3.   5 7 6 9
    + 7 7 8 4
    ─────────
    1 3 5 5 3
       1 1 1

4. 4758
    + 7586
    = 12344

5. 6372
    + 7896
    = 14268

6. 8765
    + 9475
    = 18240

7. 7853
    + 3746
    = 11599

8. 6482
    + 5796
    = 12278

9. 5497
    + 8625
    = 14122

10. Answers will vary.

Rocket There are several possible combinations that make the addition work, using different arrangements of the following:

9523
+ 1364
= 10887

Page 31
Adding and subtracting

1. 246 − 60 = 186 miles
   Adjust + 1 = 187 miles
2. 427 − 80 = 347 miles
   Adjust + 1 = 348 miles
3. 154 − 90 = 64 miles
   Adjust + 2 = 66 miles
4. 285 − 80 = 205 miles
   Adjust + 1 = 206 miles
5. 274 − 60 = 214 miles
   Adjust + 3 = 217 miles
6. 164 − 90 = 74 miles
   Adjust + 1 = 75 miles
7. 247 − 40 = 207 cm
   Adjust + 1 = 208 cm
8. 247 − 70 = 177 cm
   Adjust + 3 = 180 cm
9. 247 − 100 = 147 cm
   Adjust + 1 = 148 cm
10. 247 − 130 = 117 cm
    Adjust + 2 = 119 cm
11. 247 − 190 = 57 cm
    Adjust + 1 = 58 cm

Rocket Answers will vary.

Page 32
Counting on and back to calculate

1. Answers may vary.
2. Answers may vary.
3. False
4. False
5. True
6. True
7. False

Rocket The answer is not always a palindrome.

Page 33
Adding

1. 5 + 95 = 100
   10 + 90 = 100
   15 + 85 = 100
   20 + 80 = 100
   25 + 75 = 100
   30 + 70 = 100
   35 + 65 = 100
   40 + 60 = 100
   45 + 55 = 100
   50 + 50 = 100
2. 65 + 5 = 70
   5 years
3. 18 + 2 = 20
   2 years
4. 27 + 3 = 30
   3 years
5. 43 + 7 = 50
   7 years
6. 32 + 8 = 40
   8 years
7. 87 + 3 = 90
   3 years
8. 51 + 9 = 60
   9 years
9. 44 + 6 = 50
   6 years

Rocket Answers may vary; the maximum is 10 different ways.

Page 34
Adding and subtracting

1. 350 + 650 = 1000 m
2. 450 + 550 = 1000 m
3. 650 + 350 = 1000 m
4. 850 + 150 = 1000 m
5. 750 + 250 = 1000 m
6. 420 + 580 = 1000 m
7. 680 + 320 = 1000 m
8. 730 + 270 = 1000 m
9. 230 + 770 = 1000 m

Rocket Answers will vary but must include three multiples of 50, for example: 500 + 400 + 100 = 1000.

10. 340 g
11. 220 ml
12. Tanvi needs £32. Her sister needs £46.

Rocket £638, £542, £329, £116

Page 35
Doubling and halving

1. 23 → 40, 6 = 46
2. 31 → 60, 2 = 62
3. 44 → 80, 8 = 88
4. 12 → 20, 4 = 24
5. 16 → 20, 12 = 32
6. 27 → 40, 14 = 54
7. 38 → 60, 16 = 76
8. 19 → 20, 18 = 38
9. 28 → 40, 16 = 56
10. 36 → 60, 12 = 72
11. 49 → 80, 18 = 98
12. 57 → 100, 14 = 114
13. 48 → 20, 4 = 24
14. 26 → 10, 3 = 13
15. 46 → 20, 3 = 23
16. 82 → 40, 1 = 41
17. 34 → 15, 2 = 17
18. 58 → 25, 4 = 29
19. 76 → 35, 3 = 38

20. 38 / 15 4 = 19
21. 92 / 45 1 = 46
22. 64 / 30 2 = 32
23. 72 / 35 1 = 36
24. 54 / 25 2 = 27
25. 2 × £32 = £64
26. 2 × £48 = £96
27. 2 × £38 = £76
28. 2 × £18 = £36
29. 2 × £24 = £48

Half Price:
25. £16
26. £24
27. £19
28. £9
29. £12

Rocket
25. £160
26. £240
27. £190
28. £90
29. £120

You can find the cost of 20 of each item by doubling and then multiplying by 10, or multiplying by 10 and then doubling.

Page 36
Near doubles

1. double 34 = 68
   35 + 34 = 69
2. double 42 = 84
   42 + 41 = 83
3. double 26 = 52
   26 + 27 = 53
4. double 18 = 36
   18 + 19 = 37
5. double 23 = 46
   23 + 22 = 45
6. double 45 = 90
   45 + 44 = 89
7. double 28 = 56
   28 + 27 = 55
8. double 37 = 74
   37 + 36 = 73
9. double 46 = 92
   46 + 47 = 93
10. double 31 + 1 or double 32 − 1
11. double 15 + 1 or double 16 − 1
12. double 22 + 1 or double 23 − 1
13. double 14 + 1 or double 15 − 1
14. double 43 + 1 or double 44 − 1
15. double 26 + 1 or double 27 − 1
16. double 35 + 1 or double 36 − 1
17. double 47 + 1 or double 48 − 1
18. 18
19. 48
20. 14
21. 62

Rocket Answers will vary.

Page 37
Using doubles and halves

1. 13 × 100 = 1300
   13 × 50 = 650
2. 22 × 100 = 2200
   22 × 50 = 1100
3. 38 × 100 = 3800
   38 × 50 = 1900
4. 17 × 100 = 1700
   17 × 50 = 850
5. 41 × 100 = 4100
   41 × 50 = 2050
6. 27 × 100 = 2700
   27 × 50 = 1350
7. 35 × 100 = 3500
   35 × 50 = 1750
8. 19 × 100 = 1900
   19 × 50 = 950
9. 24 × 100 = 2400
   24 × 50 = 1200
10. 16 × 100 = 1600
    16 × 50 = 800
    16 × 25 = 400
11. 34 × 100 = 3400
    34 × 50 = 1700
    34 × 25 = 850
12. 28 × 100 = 2800
    28 × 50 = 1400
    28 × 25 = 700
13. 22 × 100 = 2200
    22 × 50 = 1100
    22 × 25 = 550
14. 36 × 100 = 3600
    36 × 50 = 1800
    36 × 25 = 900
15. 44 × 100 = 4400
    44 × 50 = 2200
    44 × 25 = 1100
16. 58 × 100 = 5800
    58 × 50 = 2900
    58 × 25 = 1450
17. 64 × 100 = 6400
    64 × 50 = 3200
    64 × 25 = 1600
18. 72 × 100 = 7200
    72 × 50 = 3600
    72 × 25 = 1800

Rocket Children's methods may vary. One method is to multiply by 3, then by 100, then halve.

Page 38
Adding

1. 836 + 342 = 1178
2. 778 + 564 = 1342
3. 564 + 657 = 1221
4. 778 + 342 = 1120
5. Jamie and Ling had the largest score: 1614.
6. Kulpreet and Emma had the lowest score: 906.
7. 4650 + 3725 = 8375
8. 5671 + 3157 = 8828
9. 3712 + 2834 = 6546
10. 6172 + 2519 = 8691
11. 4384 + 3575 = 7959
12. 3942 + 1436 = 5378
13. 6742 + 2637 = 9379
14. 4235 + 3417 = 7652

Rocket

6363 + 3637 = 10000

Page 39
Adding

1. (13000)
   ```
     3578
   + 8675
   -----
   12253
   ```

2. (7200)
   ```
     6995
   +  218
   -----
    7213
   ```

3. (9000)
   ```
     3443
   + 6354
   -----
    9797
   ```

4. (17000)
   ```
     7668
   + 8985
   -----
   16653
   ```

Rocket Largest total is 16 173
Smallest is 3825
Largest even total is 16 164
Smallest even total is 3834

5.
   ```
     4783
   + 5878
   -----
   10661
   ```
   Ten thousand, six hundred and sixty-one

6.
   ```
     6786
   + 8595
   -----
   15381
   ```
   Fifteen thousand, three hundred and eighty-one

7.
   ```
     3642
   + 6272
   -----
    9914
   ```
   Nine thousand, nine hundred and fourteen

8.
   ```
     8872
   + 3569
   -----
   12441
   ```
   Twelve thousand, four hundred and forty-one

9.
   ```
     7535
   + 8169
   -----
   15704
   ```
   Fifteen thousand, seven hundred and four

10.
    ```
      1368
    + 9453
    -----
    10821
    ```
    Ten thousand, eight hundred and twenty-one

Page 40
Subtracting

1.
   ```
     372
   - 168
   -----
     204 miles
   ```

2.
   ```
     683
   - 329
   -----
     354 miles
   ```

3.
   ```
     492
   - 227
   -----
     265 miles
   ```

4.
   ```
     871
   - 436
   -----
     435 miles
   ```

5.
   ```
     683
   - 325
   -----
     358 miles
   ```

6.
   ```
     792
   - 244
   -----
     548 miles
   ```

7.
   ```
     983
   - 826
   -----
     157 miles
   ```

8.
   ```
     674
   - 238
   -----
     436 miles
   ```

9.
   ```
     462
   - 219
   -----
     243 miles
   ```

10.
    ```
      816
    - 542
    -----
      274 m
    ```

11.
    ```
      807
    - 261
    -----
      646 m
    ```

12.
    ```
      828
    - 453
    -----
      375 m
    ```

13.
    ```
      719
    - 256
    -----
      463 m
    ```

14.
    ```
      836
    - 382
    -----
      454 m
    ```

15.
    ```
      948
    - 295
    -----
      653 m
    ```

16.
    ```
      827
    - 586
    -----
      241 m
    ```

17.
    ```
      639
    - 265
    -----
      374 m
    ```

Rocket 799

Page 41
Adding

1.
   ```
     4683
      742
     3604
   +   28
   -----
     9057
   ```

2.
   ```
     3568
       47
   +  362
   -----
     3977
   ```

3.
   ```
     1462
      556
       98
   + 1134
   -----
     3250
   ```

4.
   ```
     2673
      843
       62
   +  359
   -----
     3937
   ```

5.
   ```
     6437
      362
       12
   + 1794
   -----
     8605
   ```

6.
```
     38
    691
   3742
 + 6438
 ―――――
  10909
    121
```

7. Answers will vary.
Rocket Answers will vary.

Page 42
Subtracting

1.
```
  54³²2
 - 2118
 ―――――
   3314
```

2.
```
  4⁷8²6
 - 1452
 ―――――
   3374
```

3.
```
  6⁰7¹¹2¹8
 - 4029
 ―――――
   2099
```

4.
```
  ⁶7¹269
 - 3542
 ―――――
   3727
```

5.
```
  7⁵6¹36
 - 2172
 ―――――
   5464
```

6.
```
  65⁷8¹3
 - 4128
 ―――――
   2455
```

7.
```
  ⁴5¹296
 - 2734
 ―――――
   2562
```

8.
```
  48²3¹1
 - 3614
 ―――――
   1217
```

9.
```
  ²3¹175
 - 1432
 ―――――
   1743 km
```
One thousand, seven hundred and forty-three kilometres

10.
```
  56³4¹7
 - 2518
 ―――――
   3129 km
```
Three thousand, one hundred and twenty-nine kilometres

11.
```
  9⁵6¹28
 - 4361
 ―――――
   5267 km
```
Five thousand, two hundred and sixty-seven kilometres

12.
```
  ⁷8¹496
 - 3753
 ―――――
   4743 km
```
Four thousand, seven hundred and forty-three kilometres

13.
```
  7⁵6¹32
 - 3271
 ―――――
   4361 km
```
Four thousand, three hundred and sixty-one kilometres

14.
```
  94²3¹8
 - 2219
 ―――――
   7219 km
```
Seven thousand, two hundred and nineteen kilometres

15.
```
  ⁴5¹296
 - 2534
 ―――――
   2762 km
```
Two thousand, seven hundred and sixty-two kilometres

16.
```
  8⁵6¹35
 - 5272
 ―――――
   3363 km
```
Three thousand, three hundred and sixty-three kilometres

Rocket 8765 − 1234 gives the largest possible answer of 7531.

Page 43
Subtracting

1.
```
  £⁴A²8⁷¹4
 - £  768
 ―――――
   £3516
```

2.
```
  £5⁴5⁰¹6
 - £1285
 ―――――
   £4221
```

3.
```
  £⁴A³8⁷¹1
 - £2816
 ―――――
   £1565
```

4.
```
  £³A⁶7⁰6
 - £1375
 ―――――
   £2331
```

5.
```
  £²3⁵¹⁴27
 - £1643
 ―――――
   £1884
```

6.
```
  £⁶7⁶³A⁵5
 - £  837
 ―――――
   £6808
```

7.
```
  £⁴5⁴¹³A⁵6³
 - £  976
 ―――――
   £4487
```

8.
```
  £7⁸9⁷A⁵
 - £3697
 ―――――
   £4288
```

9.
```
  £⁵6⁴⁶7¹3
 - £5728
 ―――――
   £  745
```

10.
```
  £⁴5⁴³²A¹2
 - £  683
 ―――――
   £4659
```

11.
```
  £⁷8³⁷²A⁵5
 - £2348
 ―――――
   £3487
```

12.
```
  £⁵6⁴¹³A7
 - £  892
 ―――――
   £5545
```

Rocket Answers will vary.

13.
```
  5²3¹4⁷¹6
 - 2817
 ―――――
   50329
```

14.
```
  ²3¹8⁷¹1
 - 1976
 ―――――
   1905
```

15.
```
  6³A⁶3⁷¹8
 - 2769
 ―――――
   61609
```

16.
```
  ⁴5¹³A²8⁶
 - 1787
 ―――――
   3649
```

17.
$$\begin{array}{r} 3\,\overset{2}{\cancel{3}}\,\overset{11}{\cancel{2}}\,\overset{15}{\cancel{6}}\,\overset{1}{5} \\ -\ 1\ 6\ 7\ 8 \\ \hline 3\ 1\ 5\ 8\ 7 \end{array}$$

18.
$$\begin{array}{r} \overset{5}{\cancel{6}}\,\overset{1}{3}\,\overset{7}{\cancel{8}}\,\overset{1}{4} \\ -\ 2\ 6\ 3\ 7 \\ \hline 3\ 7\ 4\ 7 \end{array}$$

Page 44
Subtracting

1. 836 m
2. 27 m
3. 783 m
4. 305 m
5. 504 m
6. 1115 m
7. 810 m
8. 531 m
9. 332 m
10. 279 m

Rocket Answers will vary.

11. 46 831 − 7994 = 38 837
12. 5218 − 3961 = 1257
13. 7654 − 379 = 7275
14. 64 382 − 5317 = 59 065
15. 47 932 − 8364 = 39 568
16. 6431 − 3786 = 2645
17. 32 465 − 6374 = 26 091
18. 4261 − 1794 = 2467
19. 47 653 − 24 278 = 23 375
20. 22 643 − 1875 = 20 768
21. 34 652 − 26 741 = 7911
22. 18 567 − 9379 = 9188

Page 45
Multiplying

1. (20 × 5) + (5 × 3)
   = 100 + 15
   = 115
2. (50 × 7) + (2 × 7)
   = 350 + 14
   = 364
3. (100 × 4) − (1 × 4)
   = 400 − 4
   = 396
4. (100 × 6) + (1 × 6)
   = 600 + 6
   = 606
5. (50 × 3) + (1 × 3)
   = 150 + 3
   = 153
6. (50 × 8) − (1 × 8)
   = 400 − 8
   = 392
7. 23 × 10 = 230
   23 × 9 = 230 − 23
   = 207 points in a season
8. 13 × 10 = 130
   13 × 8 = 130 − 26
   = 104 shots on target
9. 4 × 50 = 200
   4 × 49 = 200 − 4
   = 196
10. 6 × 50 = 300
    6 × 49 = 300 − 6
    = 294

11. 7 × 50 = 350
    7 × 49 = 350 − 7
    = 343
12. 2 × 50 = 100
    2 × 49 = 100 − 2
    = 98
13. 9 × 50 = 450
    9 × 49 = 450 − 9
    = 441
14. 8 × 50 = 400
    8 × 49 = 400 − 8
    = 392
15. 3 × 50 = 150
    3 × 49 = 150 − 3
    = 147
16. 5 × 50 = 250
    5 × 49 = 250 − 5
    = 245
17. 11 × 50 = 550
    11 × 49 = 550 − 11
    = 539

Page 46
Multiplying by multiples of 10

1. 1200 m
2. 1600 m
3. 2400 m
4. 2800 m
5. 800 m
6. 3600 m

Rocket
1. 2400 m
2. 3200 m
3. 4800 m
4. 5600 m
5. 1600 m
6. 7200 m

Each car travels twice as far as before.

7. 30 × 50 = 1500
8. 40 × 70 = 2800
9. 200 × 30 = 6000
10. 300 × 70 = 21 000
11. 500 × 60 = 30 000
12. 800 × 50 = 40 000

Rocket Answers will vary.

Page 47
Multiplying

1.
	30	7
5	150	35

   150
   + 35

   185

   5 × 37 = 185

2.
	40	3
6	240	18

   240
   + 18

   258

   6 × 43 = 258

3.
	20	8
3	60	24

   60
   + 24

   84

   3 × 28 = 84

4.
	70	2
4	280	8

   280
   + 8

   288

   4 × 72 = 288

5.
	30	4
8	240	32

   240
   + 32

   272

   8 × 34 = 272

6.
	40	2
9	360	18

   360
   + 18

   378

   9 × 42 = 378

7. estimate: 3 × 30 = 90
	20	7
3	60	21

   3 × 27 = 81

8. estimate: 4 × 40 = 160
	40	3
4	160	12

   4 × 43 = 172

9. estimate: 5 × 40 = 200
	30	8
5	150	40

   5 × 38 = 190

10. estimate 6 × 70 = 420
	70	4
6	420	24

    6 × 74 = 444

11. estimate 7 × 30 = 210
	30	3
7	210	21

    7 × 33 = 231

12. estimate: 8 × 30 = 240
	20	9
8	160	72

    8 × 29 = 232

Rocket Answers will vary.
Possible answers include:
9 × 26 = 234
8 × 29 = 232
7 × 34 = 238
6 × 39 = 234
5 × 47 = 235
4 × 59 = 236
3 × 79 = 237

Page 48

Multiplying

1.

×	40	200	60	700	90	300
5	200	1000	300	3500	450	1500
7	280	1400	420	4900	630	2100
3	120	600	180	2100	270	900
8	320	1600	480	5600	720	2400

Rocket Answers will vary.

2. 3 × |600|210|15| (200 70 5)
    600
    210
    + 15
    825
    275 × 3 = 825

3. 4 × |1200|160|8| (300 40 2)
    1200
    160
    + 8
    1368
    342 × 4 = 1368

4. 5 × |2000|100|15| (400 20 3)
    2000
    100
    + 15
    2115
    423 × 5 = 2115

5. 3 × |600|300|48| (100 50 8)
    600
    300
    + 48
    948
    158 × 6 = 948

6. 5 × |2000|150|45| (400 30 9)
    2000
    150
    + 45
    2195
    439 × 5 = 2195

7. 2 × |1200|20|16| (600 10 8)
    1200
    20
    + 16
    1236
    618 × 2 = 1236

8. 4 × |800|240|16| (200 60 4)
    800
    240
    + 16
    1056
    264 × 4 = 1056

9. 4 × |1200|360|28| (300 90 7)
    1200
    360
    + 28
    1588
    397 × 4 = 1588

10. 3 × |1500|180|3| (500 60 1)
    1500
    180
    + 3
    1683
    561 × 3 = 1683

11. 3 × |2400|480|12| (400 80 2)
    2400
    480
    + 12
    2892
    482 × 3 = 2892

12. 5 × |1000|350|45| (200 70 9)
    1000
    350
    + 45
    1395
    279 × 5 = 1395

13. 2 × |1600|80|10| (800 40 5)
    1600
    80
    + 10
    1690
    845 × 2 = 1690

14. 4 × |2400|200|36| (600 50 9)
    2400
    200
    + 36
    2636
    659 × 4 = 2636

15. 3 × |900|150|12| (300 50 4)
    900
    150
    + 12
    1062
    354 × 3 = 1062

16. 6 × |2400|60|30| (400 10 5)
    2400
    60
    + 30
    2490
    415 × 6 = 2490

Page 49

Multiplying

1. Incorrect: 348 × 6 = 2088
2. Correct
3. Incorrect: 238 × 7 = 1666
4. Incorrect: 618 × 5 = 3090
5. Incorrect: 279 × 7 = 1953
6. Correct
7. Incorrect: 597 × 4 = 2388
8. Incorrect: 592 × 3 = 1776
9. Correct

Rocket Padma is correct. James probably multiplied 4 by 6, instead of 40.

10. 1672
11. 2660
12. 2842
13. 5640
14. 1410
15. 2432
16. 4536
17. 1228
18. 6320
19. 972 cm wide; 28 cm left to fill.

Page 50

Multiplying

1. 86
    × 6
    480   6 × 80
    36   6 × 6
    516
    £516

2. 32
    × 3
    90   3 × 30
    6   3 × 2
    96
    £96

3. 47
    × 4
    160   4 × 40
    28   4 × 7
    188
    £188

4. 43
    × 2
    80   2 × 40
    6   2 × 3
    86
    £86

5. 58
    × 6
    300   6 × 50
    48   6 × 8
    348
    £348

6. 63
    × 3
    180   3 × 60
    9   3 × 3
    189
    £189

7. 74
    × 7
    490
    28
    518
    £518

8. 28
    × 4
    80
    32
    112
    £112

9. 24
    × 2
    40
    8
    48
    £48

Rocket Largest answers: 54 × 6 = 324;
87 × 9 = 783
Smallest answers: 45 × 3 = 135;
78 × 6 = 468

Page 51
Multiplying

1. ⓐ900
   ```
     3 1 4
   ×     3
   ─────────
     9 0 0   3 × 300
       3 0   3 × 10
       1 2   3 × 4
   ─────────
     9 4 2
   ```

2. ⓐ800
   ```
     1 8 6
   ×     4
   ─────────
     4 0 0   4 × 100
     3 2 0   4 × 80
       2 4   4 × 6
   ─────────
     7 4 4
   ```

3. ⓐ1600
   ```
     7 8 6
   ×     2
   ─────────
     1 4 0 0   2 × 700
       1 6 0   2 × 80
         1 2   2 × 6
   ─────────
     1 5 7 2
   ```

4. ⓐ1500
   ```
     2 7 4
   ×     5
   ─────────
     1 0 0 0   5 × 200
       3 5 0   5 × 70
         2 0   5 × 4
   ─────────
     1 3 7 0
   ```

5. ⓐ1800
   ```
     3 2 7
   ×     6
   ─────────
     1 8 0 0   6 × 300
       1 2 0   6 × 20
         4 2   6 × 7
   ─────────
     1 9 6 2
   ```

6. ⓐ3600
   ```
     6 4 3
   ×     6
   ─────────
     3 6 0 0   6 × 600
       2 4 0   6 × 40
         1 8   6 × 3
   ─────────
     3 8 5 8
   ```

7. ⓐ1500
   ```
     5 1 2
   ×     3
   ─────────
     1 5 0 0   3 × 500
         3 0   3 × 10
          6    3 × 2
   ─────────
     1 5 3 6
   ```

8. ⓐ2000
   ```
     4 8 7
   ×     4
   ─────────
     1 6 0 0   4 × 400
       3 2 0   4 × 80
         2 8   4 × 7
   ─────────
     1 9 4 8
   ```

9. ⓐ800
   ```
     3 5 6
   ×     2
   ─────────
     6 0 0   2 × 300
     1 0 0   2 × 50
       1 2   2 × 6
   ─────────
     7 1 2
   ```

10. ⓐ1200
    ```
      2 7 4
    ×     4
    ─────────
      8 0 0   4 × 200
      2 8 0   4 × 70
        1 6   4 × 4
    ─────────
    1 0 9 6
    ```

11. ⓐ1200
    ```
      5 6 3
    ×     2
    ─────────
    1 0 0 0   2 × 500
      1 2 0   2 × 60
          6   2 × 3
    ─────────
    1 1 2 6
    ```

12. ⓐ1200
    ```
      6 2 3
    ×     2
    ─────────
    1 2 0 0   2 × 600
        4 0   2 × 20
          6   2 × 3
    ─────────
    1 2 4 6
    ```

13. ⓐ1800
    ```
      3 3 5
    ×     6
    ─────────
    1 8 0 0   6 × 300
      1 8 0   6 × 30
        3 0   6 × 5
    ─────────
    2 0 1 0
    ```

14. ⓐ1200
    ```
      4 2 2
    ×     3
    ─────────
    1 2 0 0   3 × 400
        6 0   3 × 20
          6   3 × 2
    ─────────
    1 2 6 6
    ```

15. a: £1384
    b: £1730
    c: £2422
16. a: £2172
    b: £2715
    c: £3801
17. a: £944
    b: £1180
    c: £1652
18. a: £1272
    b: £1590
    c: £2226
19. a: £1096
    b: £1370
    c: £1918
20. a: £1748
    b: £2185
    c: £3059

Rocket Answers will vary but include:
324 × 2 = 648; 216 × 3 = 648;
162 × 4 = 648.

Page 52
Multiplying

1. ⓐ1500
   ```
     5 2 8
   ×     3
   ─────────
   1 5 0 0
       6 0
       2 4
   ─────────
   1 5 8 4
   ```

2. ⓐ2000
   ```
     4 6 4
   ×     4
   ─────────
   1 6 0 0
     2 4 0
       1 6
   ─────────
   1 8 5 6
   ```

3. ⓐ4200
   ```
     7 3 2
   ×     6
   ─────────
   4 2 0 0
     1 8 0
       1 2
   ─────────
   4 3 9 2
   ```

4. ⓐ1200
   ```
     3 2 6
   ×     4
   ─────────
       2 4
       8 0
   1 2 0 0
   ─────────
   1 3 0 4
   ```

5. ⓐ1500
   ```
     4 5 8
   ×     3
   ─────────
   1 2 0 0
     1 5 0
       2 4
   ─────────
   1 3 7 4
   ```

6. ⓐ4200
   ```
     7 2 4
   ×     6
   ─────────
   4 2 0 0
     1 2 0
       2 4
   ─────────
   4 3 4 4
   ```

Whole Number Pupil Book 1

7. (2400)

562
× 4
2000
240
8
2248

8. (2000)

395
× 5
1500
450
25
1975

9. (2400)

643
× 4
2400
160
12
2572

10. (3500)

527
× 7
3500
140
49
3689

11. (2100)

741
× 3
2100
120
3
2223

12. 1704 boxes
13. 592 boxes
14. 1104 boxes
15. 1300 boxes
16. 2168 boxes
17. 1764 boxes

Rocket
12. £106·50
13. £37·00
14. £69·00
15. £81·25
16. £135·50
17. £110·25

Page 53

Multiplying

1.

276
× 3
600 3 × 200
210 3 × 70
18 3 × 6
828

276
× 3
828
2 1

2.

436
× 4
1744

3.

147
× 6
882

4.

382
× 6
2292

5.

247
× 5
1235

6.

523
× 3
1569

7.

193
× 6
1158

8.

318
× 7
2226

9. £11
10. £178 for 6 months.

Rocket Largest number: 543 × 6 = 3258
Smallest number: 456 × 3 = 1368
Numbers between 2000 and 3000: 2124, 2144, 2180, 2252, 2315, 2540, 2610, 2612, 2718

Page 54

Multiplying

1.

	30	2
20	600	40
7	210	14

640
+ 224
£864

2. £756
3. £1848
4. £1056
5. £2583
6. £696
7. £1064
8. £1092
9. £1836
10. True
11. True
12. False
13. True

Page 55

Multiplying

1.

	200	30	8
20	4000	600	160
4	800	120	32

4760
+ 952
£5712
1 1

2. £149 × 28 = £4172
3. £117 × 23 = £2691
4. £137 × 18 = £2466
5. £246 × 25 = £6150
6. £324 × 19 = £6156

Rocket Answers will vary.
7. 427 × 21 = 8967
8. 316 × 32 = 10 112
9. 235 × 43 = 10 105
10. 547 × 54 = 29 538
11. 189 × 26 = 4914
12. 237 × 33 = 7821
13. 347 × 48 = 16 656
14. 526 × 29 = 15 254
15. 637 × 36 = 22 932
16. 483 × 23 = 11 109
17. 615 × 44 = 27 060
18. 384 × 21 = 8064

Page 56

Multiplying

1. 274 × 23

	200	70	4
20	4000	1400	80
3	600	210	12

5480
+ 822
6302

2. 156 × 32

	100	50	6
30	3000	1500	180
2	200	100	12

4680
+ 312
4992

3. 326 × 18

	300	20	8
10	8000	600	60
8	2400	160	48

3260
+ 2608
5868

4. 438 × 26

	400	50	6
20	8000	600	160
6	2400	180	48

8760
+ 2628
11388

5. 267 × 34

	200	60	7
30	6000	1800	210
4	800	240	28

8010
+ 1068
9078

6. 213 × 14 = 2982
7. 652 × 23 = 14 996
8. 821 × 32 = 26 272
9. 734 × 26 = 19 084
10. 513 × 19 = 9747
11. 525 × 24 = 12 600

Rocket Answers may vary. Rounding each distance to the nearest hundred miles we can say that, to cover 5000 miles takes approximately:

6. 25 trips
7. 7 trips
8. 6 trips
9. 7 trips
10. 10 trips
11. 10 trips

Page 57
Multiplying

1. 20 × 30 = 600
2. 40 × 30 = 1200
3. 40 × 20 = 800
4. 50 × 20 = 1000
5. (800)
   ```
       4 3
   ×   1 8
   -------
     3 4 4   43 × 8
     4 3 0   43 × 10
   -------
     7 7 4
   ```
6. (800)
   ```
       3 7
   ×   2 3
   -------
     1 1 1   37 × 3
     7 4 0   37 × 20
   -------
     8 5 1
   ```
7. (1800)
   ```
       5 6
   ×   3 3
   -------
     1 6 8   56 × 3
     1 6 8 0 56 × 30
   -------
     1 8 4 8
   ```
8.
   ```
       5 3
   ×   1 6
   -------
     8 4 8
   ```
9.
   ```
       4 7
   ×   2 2
   -------
     1 0 3 4
   ```
10.
   ```
       3 9
   ×   3 3
   -------
     1 2 8 7
   ```
11.
   ```
       5 2
   ×   1 9
   -------
     9 8 8
   ```
12. 256 sweets left
13. 232 weeks
14. 1728 cm; 272 cm

Rocket Answers will vary.

Page 58
Multiplying

1. (1500)
   ```
       4 6
   ×   2 7
   -------
     1 2 4 2
   ```
2. (900)
   ```
       2 8
   ×   3 4
   -------
     9 5 2
   ```
3. (1800)
   ```
       5 6
   ×   2 9
   -------
     1 6 2 4
   ```
4. (2000)
   ```
       5 2
   ×   4 3
   -------
     2 2 3 6
   ```
5. (1200)
   ```
       2 8
   ×   3 7
   -------
     1 0 3 6
   ```
6. (1000)
   ```
       5 3
   ×   1 7
   -------
     9 0 1
   ```
7. (1800)
   ```
       6 4
   ×   2 7
   -------
     1 7 2 8
   ```
8. (1800)
   ```
       6 3
   ×   3 2
   -------
     2 0 1 6
   ```
9. 468 m²
10. 805 m²
11. 1161 m²
12. 3528 m²

Rocket Answers will vary.

Page 59
Dividing using 10s

1.
   ```
       7 5
   -   5 0   (10) × 5
   -------
       2 5
   -   2 5   (5) × 5
   -------
         0
   ```
   75 ÷ 5 = 15 r 0

2.
   ```
       4 9
   -   3 0   (10) × 3
   -------
       1 9
   -   1 8   (6) × 4
   -------
         1
   ```
   49 ÷ 3 = 16 r 1

3.
   ```
       5 2
   -   4 0   (10) × 4
   -------
       1 2
   -   1 2   (3) × 4
   -------
         0
   ```
   52 ÷ 4 = 13

4.
   ```
       4 2
   -   3 0   (10) × 3
   -------
       1 2
   -   1 2   (4) × 3
   -------
         0
   ```
   42 ÷ 3 = 14

5.
   ```
       5 6
   -   4 0   (10) × 4
   -------
       1 6
   -   1 6   (4) × 4
   -------
         0
   ```
   56 ÷ 4 = 14

6.
   ```
       8 5
   -   5 0   (10) × 5
   -------
       3 5
   -   3 5   (7) × 5
   -------
         0
   ```
   85 ÷ 5 = 17

7.
   ```
       4 2
   -   2 0   (10) × 2
   -------
       2 2
   -   2 0   (10) × 2
   -------
         2
   -     2   (1) × 2
   -------
         0
   ```
   42 ÷ 2 = 21

8.
   ```
       3 9
   -   3 0   (10) × 3
   -------
         9
   -     9   (3) × 3
   -------
         0
   ```
   39 ÷ 3 = 13

9.
   ```
       9 6
   -   3 0   (10) × 3
   -------
       6 6
   -   3 0   (10) × 3
   -------
       3 6
   -   3 0   (10) × 3
   -------
         6
   -     6   (2) × 3
   -------
         0
   ```
   96 ÷ 3 = 32

10.
   ```
       7 9
   -   4 0   (10) × 4
   -------
       3 9
   -   3 6   (9) × 4
   -------
         3
   ```
   79 ÷ 4 = 19 r 3

Rocket Half of 64 is 32. There are 8 fours in 32. Double 32 is 64 and double 8 is 16 so there must be 16 fours in 64.

10. 12 cards
11. 14 children

Page 60
Dividing

1. $\begin{array}{r} 9\,6 \\ -6\,0 \\ \hline 3\,6 \\ -3\,6 \\ \hline 0 \end{array}$ ⑩ × 6
   ⑥ × 6

   96 ÷ 6 = 16

2. $\begin{array}{r} 8\,5 \\ -5\,0 \\ \hline 3\,5 \\ -3\,5 \\ \hline 0 \end{array}$ ⑩ × 5
   ⑦ × 5

   85 ÷ 5 = 17

3. $\begin{array}{r} 7\,8 \\ -6\,0 \\ \hline 1\,8 \\ -1\,8 \\ \hline 0 \end{array}$ ⑩ × 6
   ③ × 6

   78 ÷ 6 = 13

4. $\begin{array}{r} 8\,4 \\ -7\,0 \\ \hline 1\,4 \\ -1\,4 \\ \hline 0 \end{array}$ ⑩ × 7
   ② × 7

   84 ÷ 7 = 12

5. $\begin{array}{r} 9\,6 \\ -8\,0 \\ \hline 1\,6 \\ -1\,6 \\ \hline 0 \end{array}$ ⑩ × 8
   ② × 8

   96 ÷ 8 = 12

6. $\begin{array}{r} 5\,4 \\ -3\,0 \\ \hline 2\,4 \\ -2\,4 \\ \hline 0 \end{array}$ ⑩ × 3
   ⑧ × 3

   54 ÷ 3 = 18

7. $\begin{array}{r} 7\,6 \\ -4\,0 \\ \hline 3\,6 \\ -3\,6 \\ \hline 0 \end{array}$ ⑩ × 4
   ⑨ × 4

   76 ÷ 4 = 19

8. $\begin{array}{r} 9\,2 \\ -4\,0 \\ \hline 5\,2 \\ -4\,0 \\ \hline 1\,2 \\ -1\,2 \\ \hline 0 \end{array}$ ⑩ × 4
   ⑩ × 4
   ③ × 4

   92 ÷ 4 = 23

9. $\begin{array}{r} 6\,4 \\ -4\,0 \\ \hline 2\,4 \\ -2\,4 \\ \hline 0 \end{array}$ ⑩ × 4
   ⑥ × 4

   64 ÷ 4 = 16

Rocket 80, 88, 96. All of these can also be divided equally by 1, 2 and 4.

10. 95 ÷ 5 = 19
11. 57 ÷ 3 = 19
12. 69 ÷ 3 = 23
13. 75 ÷ 3 = 25
14. 56 ÷ 2 = 28
15. 92 ÷ 4 = 23

Page 61
Remainders

1. 75 ÷ 4 = 18 r 3
2. 39 ÷ 2 = 19 r 1
3. 47 ÷ 3 = 15 r 2
4. 58 ÷ 5 = 11 r 3
5. 97 ÷ 6 = 16 r 1
6. 54 ÷ 5 = 10 r 4
7. 37 ÷ 7 = 5 r 2
8. 67 ÷ 3 = 22 r 1
9. 74 ÷ 3 = 24 r 2
10. There are 8 tulips in each row, with 2 left over.
11. 87 ÷ 5 = 17 r 2
12. 55 ÷ 3 = 18 r 1
19. 79 ÷ 4 = 19 r 3
14. 73 ÷ 3 = 24 r 1
15. 58 ÷ 8 = 7 r 2
16. 86 ÷ 4 = 21 r 2

Rocket A number is divisible by 2 when the number is even.
A number is divisible by 5 when the number ends in 5 or 0.
A number is divisible by 10 when the number ends in 0.
A number is divisible by 3 when the sum of digits is also divisible by 3.
A number is divisible by 9 when the sum of digits is 9.

Page 62
Dividing

1. $\begin{array}{r} 1\,2 \\ 4\overline{)4\,8} \\ 4\,0 \\ \hline 8 \\ \hline 0 \end{array}$ ⑩ × 4
   ② × 4

2. $\begin{array}{r} 1\,7 \\ 5\overline{)8\,5} \\ 5\,0 \\ \hline 3\,5 \\ \hline 0 \end{array}$ ⑩ × 5
   ⑦ × 5

3. $\begin{array}{r} 1\,7 \\ 3\overline{)5\,1} \\ 3\,0 \\ \hline 2\,1 \\ \hline 0 \end{array}$ ⑩ × 3
   ⑦ × 3

4. $\begin{array}{r} 1\,2 \\ 8\overline{)9\,6} \\ 8\,0 \\ \hline 1\,6 \\ \hline 0 \end{array}$ ⑩ × 8
   ② × 8

5. 16 days
   $\begin{array}{r} 3\overline{)4\,8} \\ 3\,0 \\ \hline 1\,8 \\ \hline 0 \end{array}$ ⑩ × 3
   ⑥ × 3

6. 18 days
   $\begin{array}{r} 3\overline{)5\,4} \\ 3\,0 \\ \hline 2\,4 \\ \hline 0 \end{array}$ ⑩ × 3
   ⑧ × 3

7. 19 days
   $\begin{array}{r} 3\overline{)5\,7} \\ 3\,0 \\ \hline 2\,7 \\ \hline 0 \end{array}$ ⑩ × 3
   ⑨ × 3

Rocket
5. 12 days
6. 13 days, with 2 meals left.
7. 14 days, with 1 meal left.

Page 63
Dividing

Rocket 33 ÷ 8 = 4 r 1 so 33 pages at 8 pages a day rounds up to 5 days.

1. $\begin{array}{r} 1\,8 \\ 4\overline{)7\,2} \\ 4\,0 \\ \hline 3\,2 \\ \hline 0 \end{array}$ ⑩ × 4
   ⑧ × 4

   18 days

2. $\begin{array}{r} 1\,7 \\ 3\overline{)5\,1} \\ 3\,0 \\ \hline 2\,1 \\ \hline 0 \end{array}$ ⑩ × 3
   ⑦ × 3

   17 days

3. $\begin{array}{r} 1\,4 \\ 6\overline{)8\,4} \\ 6\,0 \\ \hline 2\,4 \\ \hline 0 \end{array}$ ⑩ × 6
   ④ × 6

   14 days

4. $\begin{array}{r} 2\,4\ r2 \\ 4\overline{)9\,8} \\ 8\,0 \\ \hline 1\,6 \\ \hline 2 \end{array}$ ⑳ × 4
   ④ × 4

   25 days

5.
```
   2 8 r1
3)8 5
   6 0   (20) × 3
   2 4   (8) × 3
     1
```
29 days

6. Person 1: 72 ÷ 8 = 9
   9 days
   Person 2: 51 ÷ 8 = 6 r 3
   7 days
   Person 3: 84 ÷ 8 = 10 r 4
   11 days
   Person 4: 98 ÷ 8 = 12 r 2
   13 days
   Person 5: 85 ÷ 8 = 10 r 5
   11 days

A quick way to work out how long Person 1 and Person 4 will take is to halve their previous numbers of days.

Page 64
Dividing

1.
```
      3 4 r2
4)1 3 8
   1 2 0   (30) × 4
     1 8
     1 6   (4) × 4
       2
```

2.
```
      3 9 r1
5)1 9 6
   1 5 0   (30) × 5
     4 6
     4 5   (9) × 5
       1
```

3.
```
      4 4 r3
5)2 2 3
   2 0 0   (40) × 5
     2 3
     2 0   (4) × 5
       3
```

4–12. Children's choice as to the 'chunks' to subtract may vary.

4. 191 ÷ 6 = 31 r 5
5. 173 ÷ 4 = 43 r 1
6. 221 ÷ 3 = 73 r 2
7. 316 ÷ 5 = 63 r 1
8. 190 ÷ 4 = 47 r 2
9. 487 ÷ 6 = 81 r 1
10. 363 ÷ 4 = 90 r 3
11. 284 ÷ 3 = 94 r 2
12. 367 ÷ 5 = 73 r 2
13. 165 ÷ 3 = 55, so 55 weeks
14. 233 ÷ 4 = 58 r 1, so 59 weeks
15. 191 ÷ 7 = 27 r 2, so 28 weeks
16. 346 ÷ 5 = 69 r 1, so 70 weeks
17. 213 ÷ 6 = 35 r 3, so 36 weeks
18. 471 ÷ 8 = 58 r 7, so 59 weeks

Rocket £500 at £3 a week: 500 ÷ 3 = 166 r 2, so 167 weeks
£500 at £4 a week: 500 ÷ 4 = 125, so 125 weeks
£500 at £7 a week: 500 ÷ 7 = 71 r 3, so 72 weeks
£500 at £5 a week: 500 ÷ 5 = 100, so 100 weeks
£500 at £6 a week: 500 ÷ 6 = 83 r 2, so 84 weeks
£500 at £8 a week: 500 ÷ 8 = 62 r 4, so 63 weeks

Page 65
Dividing

Estimates for questions **1–20** may vary.

1.
```
       (1 4 0)
       1 3 9 r1
4)5 5 7
   4 0 0   (100) × 4
     1 5 7
     1 2 0   (30) × 4
       3 7
       3 6   (9) × 4
         1
```

Children's choice as to the 'chunks' to subtract may vary.

2. 613 ÷ 5 = 122 r 3
3. 513 ÷ 3 = 171
4. 728 ÷ 6 = 121 r 2
5. 873 ÷ 7 = 124 r 5
6. 922 ÷ 6 = 153 r 4
7. 742 ÷ 3 = 247 r 1
8. 937 ÷ 7 = 133 r 6
9. 925 ÷ 7 = 132 r 1
10. 496 ÷ 3 = 165 r 1
11. 870 ÷ 3 = 290

Rocket One eighth of 8176 = 1022 so 1022 crackers are faulty.

12. 913 ÷ 4 = 228 r 1
13. 854 ÷ 7 = 122
14. 726 ÷ 3 = 242
15. 681 ÷ 5 = 136 r 1
16. 739 ÷ 2 = 369 r 1
17. 904 ÷ 6 = 150 r 4
18. 858 ÷ 3 = 286
19. 703 ÷ 4 = 175 r 3
20. 937 ÷ 2 = 468 r 1

Page 66
Dividing

Children's estimates and choices as to the 'chunks' to subtract may vary.

1.
```
      1 4 2 r2
3)4 2 8
   3 0 0   (100) × 3
   1 2 8
   1 2 0   (40) × 3
       8
       6   (2) × 3
       2
```

2. 573 ÷ 4 = 143 r 1
3. 826 ÷ 5 = 165 r 1
4. 464 ÷ 4 = 116
5. 578 ÷ 5 = 115 r 3
6. 369 ÷ 3 = 123
7. 106 ÷ 5 = 21 r 1
8. 432 ÷ 3 = 144
9. 517 ÷ 4 = 129 r 1
10. 643 ÷ 5 = 128 r 3
11. 974 ÷ 5 = 194 r 4
12. 588 ÷ 3 = 196
13. 724 ÷ 4 = 181
14. 537 ÷ 3 = 179
15. 821 ÷ 5 = 164 r 1
16. 627 ÷ 4 = 156 r 3

Rocket 636 ÷ 4 = 159 so normally each girl delivers 159 papers; 159 ÷ 3 = 53 so each girl delivers 53 of the sick girl's papers.

Page 67
Dividing

Children's methods to solve these calculations may vary.

1. 489 ÷ 20 = 24 r 9
2. 574 ÷ 30 = 19 r 4
3. 957 ÷ 50 = 19 r 7
4. 849 ÷ 70 = 12 r 9
5. 508 ÷ 20 = 25 r 8
6. 714 ÷ 30 = 23 r 24
7. 438 ÷ 50 = 8 r 38
8. 258 ÷ 70 = 3 r 48
9. 645 ÷ 40 = 16 r 5

Rocket She can have nine 60 cm cupboards, with 39 cm left over; or fourteen 40 cm cupboards with 19 cm left over; or nineteen 30 cm cupboards with 9 cm left over.

Answers will vary for the last question.

10. 396 ÷ 40 = 9 r 36
11. 904 ÷ 80 = 11 r 24
12. 857 ÷ 30 = 28 r 17
13. 478 ÷ 80 = 5 r 78
14. 709 ÷ 40 = 17 r 29
15. 1009 ÷ 20 = 50 r 9

Page 68
Dividing

Children's methods to solve these calculations may vary.

1. 847 ÷ 30 = 28 r 7
2. 903 ÷ 40 = 22 r 23
3. 890 ÷ 30 = 29 r 20
4. 912 ÷ 30 = 30 r 12
5. 607 ÷ 40 = 15 r 7
6. 350 ÷ 60 = 5 r 50
7. 904 ÷ 70 = 12 r 64
8. 935 ÷ 70 = 13 r 25
9. 893 ÷ 20 = 44 r 13
10. 289 ÷ 20 = 14 r 9
11. 752 ÷ 30 = 25 r 2
12. 989 ÷ 20 = 49 r 9

Rocket Children's answers will vary.
One possibility is
```
         4 9 r 4
     20)9 8 4
```

13. 29 lorries (by rounding down)
14. 33 lengths (by rounding up)

Page 69

Dividing

Children's methods to solve these calculations may vary.

1. 33 ÷ 2 = 16 r 1
2. 41 ÷ 2 = 20 r 1
3. 57 ÷ 2 = 28 r 1
4. 47 ÷ 3 = 15 r 2
5. 69 ÷ 5 = 13 r 4
6. 71 ÷ 6 = 11 r 5
7. 94 ÷ 8 = 11 r 6
8. 88 ÷ 6 = 14 r 4
9. 93 ÷ 8 = 11 r 5
10. 97 ÷ 9 = 10 r 7
11. 94 ÷ 7 = 13 r 3
12. 97 ÷ 6 = 16 r 1
13. 76 ÷ 6 = 12 boxes (rounded down)
14. 79 ÷ 6 = 13 boxes (rounded down)
15. 65 ÷ 6 = 10 boxes (rounded down)
16. 70 ÷ 6 = 11 boxes (rounded down)
17. 74 ÷ 6 = 12 boxes (rounded down)
18. 71 ÷ 6 = 11 boxes (rounded down)
19. Each dwarf got £10 and Snow White kept £5.

Rocket 19 weeks

Page 70

Dividing

Children's answers for **1–9** may differ from those given.

1. 80p ÷ 4 = 20p
2. 66p ÷ 3 = 22p
3. 100p ÷ 5 = 20p
4. 72p ÷ 6 = 12p
5. 100p ÷ 4 = 25p or 92p ÷ 4 = 23p
6. 91p ÷ 7 = 13p
7. 105p ÷ 5 = 21p
8. 120p ÷ 6 = 20p or 126p ÷ 6 = 21p
9. 160p ÷ 8 = 20p

Rocket Children's answers will vary.

10. 63 ÷ 4 = 15 r 3
11. 55 ÷ 3 = 18 r 1
12. 87 ÷ 5 = 17 r 2
13. 75 ÷ 4 = 18 r 3
14. 55 ÷ 4 = 13 r 3
15. 91 ÷ 6 = 15 r 1
16. 96 ÷ 8 = 12
17. 59 ÷ 3 = 19 r 2
18. 66 ÷ 5 = 13 r 1

Page 71

Dividing

1.
```
   2 5 r 2
5)1 2 ²7
```
or
```
   2 5 r 2
5)1 2 7
   1 0 0
   -----
     2 7
     2 5
   -----
       2
```
rounds to 26 days

2. 197 ÷ 4 = 49 r 1 rounds to 50 days
3. 188 ÷ 3 = 62 r 2 rounds to 63 days
4. 113 ÷ 6 = 18 r 5 rounds to 19 days
5. 154 ÷ 9 = 17 r 1 rounds to 18 days
6. 173 ÷ 7 = 24 r 5 rounds to 25 days
7. 129 ÷ 5 = 25 r 4 rounds to 26 days
8. 185 ÷ 8 = 23 r 1 rounds to 24 days
9. 203 ÷ 6 = 33 r 5 rounds to 34 days
10. 187 ÷ 4 = 46 r 3 rounds to 47 days
11. 206 ÷ 8 = 25 r 6 rounds to 26 days

Rocket Answers will vary.

12. 177 ÷ 3 = 59
13. 113 ÷ 4 = 28 r 1
14. 123 ÷ 5 = 24 r 3
15. 147 ÷ 6 = 24 r 3
16. 183 ÷ 7 = 26 r 1
17. 107 ÷ 4 = 26 r 3
18. 121 ÷ 5 = 24 r 1
19. 203 ÷ 8 = 25 r 3
20. 164 ÷ 3 = 54 r 2
21. 139 ÷ 6 = 23 r 1

Page 72

Dividing

1.
```
   2 9 r 1
3)8 ²8
```
2. 104 ÷ 6 = 17 r 2
3. 167 ÷ 7 = 23 r 6
4. 183 ÷ 5 = 36 r 3
5. 241 ÷ 8 = 30 r 1
6. 175 ÷ 4 = 43 r 3
7. 119 ÷ 5 = 23 r 4
8. 213 ÷ 7 = 30 r 3
9. 204 ÷ 9 = 22 r 6
10. 143 ÷ 8 = 17 r 7
11. 163 ÷ 9 = 18 r 1
12. 372 ÷ 7 = 53 r 1

Rocket The following answers are possible: 71 ÷ 3, 94 ÷ 4, 117 ÷ 5, 140 ÷ 6, 163 ÷ 7, 186 ÷ 8, 209 ÷ 9.

13. 71 ÷ 4 = 17 r 3 rounds up to 18 taxis.
14. 5 × 6 = 30
15. 143 ÷ 28 = 5 r 3 rounds up to 6 albums.
16. 165 ÷ 7 = 23 r 4 rounds down to 23 sections.

Page 73

Dividing

1.
```
   1 3 8 r 2
3)4 ¹1 ²6
```

2. 627 ÷ 5 = 125 r 2
3. 739 ÷ 4 = 184 r 3
4. 726 ÷ 3 = 242
5. 943 ÷ 4 = 235 r 3
6. 827 ÷ 3 = 275 r 2
7. 623 ÷ 5 = 124 r 3
8. 862 ÷ 4 = 215 r 2
9. 148
10. 316
11. 155
12. 256
13. 162
14. 187
15. 283
16. 146
17. 124

Rocket
9. 4440
10. 9480
11. 4650
12. 7680
13. 4860
14. 5610
15. 8490
16. 4380
17. 3720

Page 74

How do we solve it?

1. Chang has 80p.
2. Total saved: £660; Afram has £96 more than Jane.
3. 53 cards
4. 166 miles
5. The first race was 180 m longer than the second race; total distance ran: 740 m.

Rocket Total distance flown: 5727 miles; the first flight was 789 miles longer than the second flight.

Page 75

How do we solve it?

1. 1120 g
2. 142 g
3. 74 cm left, which is 39 cm less than half.
4. 615 days
5. 108 staples

Rocket 12 weeks

Page 76

How do we solve it?

1. 1030 people; 1158 people after the interval.
2. 270 feet left to climb; he will climb 484 feet in total.
3. £92
4. 334 miles
5. 61 miles

Rocket £362

Page 77

How do we solve it?

1. 18 teams; 9 matches.
2. 18 pages
3. 139 packs
10. £29·50

Rocket £37·50

Page 78

How do we solve it?

1. 117 $\frac{1}{8}$ gallons or 117 gallons and 1 pint.

2. £434·60; £260·76 more.
3. 2376 miles
4. £14 778
Rocket £468

Page 79
How do we solve it?

1. £2144 less than the £40 000 hoped for.
2. $\frac{1}{3}$ of £828 is £276; $\frac{1}{4}$ of £948 is £237; the first amount is greater than the second by £39.
3. It can do 13 392 more miles.
4. Kate's number is 838; Paul's number is 947; Paul's is larger by 109.
9. £23 573

Whole Number PPMs

PPM1
Writing numbers in words

1. Forty thousand, six hundred and twenty-seven
2. Ninety-one thousand, five hundred and fourteen
3. Twenty thousand, nine hundred and seventy-three
4. Eighty-six thousand, five hundred and forty
5. Eighty-seven thousand, six hundred and forty-nine
6. Sixty-two thousand, two hundred and eighty-five
7. Twenty thousand and ninety-five
8. Eighty-seven thousand, nine hundred and thirty-six
9. Forty thousand, four hundred and sixty-nine
10. Eighty-one thousand, six hundred and twenty-eight

PPM2
Compare numbers

1.

2742	<	8536	4812	<	8782
2271	<	7706	9344	>	8449
6182	>	4966	1439	<	3418
8432	>	1897	5275	>	2753
6849	>	6763	9419	>	6578

2. 8983, 9931, 10 190, 10 202, 10 237, 35 421, 42 019, 53 241, 54 874, 66 467, 68 987, 85 329

PPM3
Adding and subtracting multiples of 10

1. 12 − 7 = 5
   120 − 70 = 50
2. 19 + 5 = 24
   190 + 50 = 240
3. 18 − 4 = 14
   180 − 40 = 140
4. 27 + 3 = 30
   270 + 30 = 300
5. 13 − 6 = 7
   130 − 60 = 70
6. 23 + 9 = 32
   230 + 90 = 320
7. 11 + 3 = 14
   110 + 30 = 140
8. 18 − 7 = 11
   180 − 70 = 110
9. 29 − 8 = 21
   290 − 80 = 210
10. 15 − 6 = 9
    150 − 60 = 90
11. 21 − 7 = 14
    210 − 70 = 140
12. 33 − 8 = 25
    330 − 80 = 250
13. Answers will vary.

PPM4
Adding and subtracting multiples of 10

1. 340 + 60 = 400
   340 − 60 = 280
2. 470 + 80 = 550
   470 − 80 = 390
3. 530 + 70 = 600
   530 − 70 = 460
4. 630 + 50 = 680
   630 − 50 = 580
5. 750 + 40 = 790
   750 − 40 = 710
6. 890 + 30 = 920
   890 − 30 = 860
7. 620 − 80 = 540
8. 520 − 40 = 480
9. 370 − 50 = 320
10. 730 + 90 = 820
11. 880 + 70 = 950
12. 760 − 30 = 730

PPM5
Adding and subtracting multiples of 10 and 100

1. 18 + 4 = 22
   1800 + 400 = 2200
2. 24 + 7 = 31
   2400 + 700 = 3100
3. 37 + 6 = 43
   3700 + 600 = 4300
4. 22 − 6 = 16
   2200 − 600 = 1600
5. 12 − 8 = 4
   1200 − 800 = 400
6. 23 − 7 = 16
   2300 − 700 = 1600
7. 14 + 8 = 22
   1400 + 800 = 2200
8. 33 − 8 = 25
   3300 − 800 = 2500
9. 41 − 9 = 32
   4100 − 900 = 3200
10. The total amount saved is £600. Rafat has saved £180 more than Megan.
11. Jordan's garden is 220 m longer than his neighbour's. The total length of the gardens is 740 m.
12. Alastair and Sian climb 5600 feet in total. The difference between the two distances is 800 feet.

PPM6
Adding and subtracting multiples of 10 and 100

1. 1800 + 600 = 2400
2. 2100 − 400 = 1700
3. 2700 + 500 = 3200
4. 3400 − 600 = 2800
5. 1500 + 800 = 2300
6. 2200 − 700 = 1500
7. 2900 − 1200 = 1700
8. 1900 + 700 = 2600
9. Answers will vary.

PPM7
Multiplication facts

1. a. 6   b. 12   c. 18
2. d. 20   e. 50   f. 80
3. g. 20   h. 30   i. 35
4. j. 3   k. 12   l. 21
5. m. 12   n. 24
6. 3 × 2 = 6
7. 3 × 10 = 30
8. 4 × 5 = 20
9. 2 × 4 = 8
10. 4 × 3 = 12
11. 9 × 2 = 18
12. 6 × 4 = 24
13. 8 × 5 = 40
14. 6 × 5 = 30
15. 5 × 3 = 15
16. 7 × 10 = 70
17. 9 × 4 = 36

PPM8
Multiplication and division facts

1. 18 ÷ 2 = 9
2. 25 ÷ 5 = 5
3. 70 ÷ 10 = 7
4. 15 ÷ 3 = 5
5. 20 ÷ 4 = 5
6. 14 ÷ 2 = 7
7. 35 ÷ 5 = 7
8. 21 ÷ 3 = 7
9. 32 ÷ 4 = 8
10. 45 ÷ 5 = 9
11. 24 ÷ 6 = 4
12. 24 ÷ 8 = 3
13. 14 ÷ 2 = 7, 14 ÷ 7 = 2
14. 15 ÷ 3 = 5, 15 ÷ 5 = 3
15. 18 ÷ 3 = 6, 18 ÷ 6 = 3
16. 28 ÷ 7 = 4, 28 ÷ 4 = 7
17. 5 × 4 = 20, 4 × 5 = 20
18. 3 × 4 = 12, 4 × 3 = 12
19. 2 × 4 = 8, 4 × 2 = 8
20. 5 × 10 = 50, 10 × 5 = 50

PPM9
Multiplication facts

1. 4 × 5 = 20
2. 3 × 7 = 21
3. 3 × 9 = 27
4. 6 × 5 = 30
5. 5 × 8 = 40
6. 7 × 6 = 42
7. 9 × 7 = 63
8. 4 × 4 = 16
9. 6 × 6 = 36
10. 7 × 5 = 35
11. 8 × 4 = 32
12. 6 × 8 = 48
13. 9 × 6 = 54
14. 4 × 9 = 36
15. 5 × 9 = 45
16. 7 × 7 = 49
17. 4 × 7 = 28
18. 9 × 9 = 81
19. 7 × 8 = 56
20. 8 × 8 = 64

PPM10
Division facts

1. 42 ÷ 7 = 6
2. 27 ÷ 3 = 9
3. 35 ÷ 5 = 7
4. 63 ÷ 9 = 7
5. 28 ÷ 7 = 4
6. 24 ÷ 8 = 3
7. 40 ÷ 8 = 5
8. 20 ÷ 5 = 4
9. 54 ÷ 9 = 6
10. 21 ÷ 3 = 7
11. 36 ÷ 4 = 9
12. 56 ÷ 8 = 7
13. 18 ÷ 3 = 6
14. 81 ÷ 9 = 9
15. 72 ÷ 8 = 9
16. 56 ÷ 7 = 8
17. 45 ÷ 5 = 9
18. 24 ÷ 4 = 6
19. 32 ÷ 4 = 8
20. 49 ÷ 7 = 7

PPM11
Sevens

1. 3 × 7 = 21
2. 8 × 7 = 56
3. 70 ÷ 7 = 10
4. 14 ÷ 7 = 2
5. 63 ÷ 7 = 9
6. 35 ÷ 7 = 5
7. 10 × 7 = 70
8. 28 ÷ 7 = 4
9. 56 ÷ 7 = 8
10. 6 × 7 = 42
11. 7 × 7 = 49
12. 4 × 7 = 28
13. 9 × 7 = 63
14. 42 ÷ 7 = 6
15. 2 × 7 = 14
16. 21 ÷ 7 = 3
17. 49 ÷ 7 = 7
18. 5 × 7 = 35

PPM12
Table facts

1. 8 × 6 = 48
2. 21 ÷ 3 = 7
3. 4 × 7 = 28
4. 42 ÷ 6 = 7
5. 32 ÷ 4 = 8
6. 8 × 3 = 24
7. 56 ÷ 7 = 8
8. 7 × 7 = 49
9. 9 × 9 = 81
10. 45 ÷ 5 = 9
11. 72 ÷ 8 = 9
12. 5 × 4 = 20
13. 8 × 5 = 40
14. 63 ÷ 9 = 7
15. 24 ÷ 4 = 6
16. 6 × 6 = 36
17. 6 × 9 = 54
18. 27 ÷ 9 = 3
19. 35 ÷ 7 = 5
20. 8 × 8 = 64
21. 3 × 6 = 18
22. 25 ÷ 5 = 5
23. 30 ÷ 6 = 5
24. 9 × 4 = 36

PPM13
Multiplying and dividing by 10 and 100

1. 47 × 10 = 470
2. 850 ÷ 10 = 85
3. 7300 ÷ 10 = 730
4. 64 × 10 = 640
5. 9 × 100 = 900
6. 800 ÷ 100 = 8
7. 27 × 100 = 2700
8. 6300 ÷ 100 = 63
9. 83 × 10 = 830
10. 790 ÷ 10 = 79
11. 520 × 10 = 5200
12. 4320 ÷ 10 = 432
13. 180 × 100 = 18 000
14. 1300 ÷ 100 = 13
15. 84 × 100 = 8400
16. 830 × 100 = 83 000
17. 46 × 100 = 4600
18. 700 ÷ 100 = 7
19. 160 × 100 = 16 000
20. 60 000 ÷ 100 = 600

PPM14
Multiplying using table facts

1. 7 × 30 = 210
2. 9 × 40 = 360
3. 4 × 60 = 240
4. 5 × 70 = 350
5. 70 × 7 = 490
6. 80 × 3 = 240
7. 90 × 7 = 630
8. 9 × 60 = 540
9. 7 × 400 = 2800
10. 500 × 4 = 2000
11. 8 × 800 = 6400
12. 6 × 800 = 4800
13. 9 × 3000 = 27 000
14. 8 × 90 = 720
15. 700 × 6 = 4200
16. 90 × 5 = 450
17. 3 × 600 = 1800
18. 600 × 6 = 3600
19. 3 × 600 = 1800
20. 80 × 4 = 320

PPM15
Multiplying by 10 and 100

1. 450 10p coins
2. 280 10p coins
3. 3100 10p coins
4. 4500 10p coins
5. 70 10p coins
6. 35 10p coins
7. 800 1p coins
8. 3200 1p coins
9. 1500 1p coins
10. 11 000 1p coins
11. 27 000 1p coins
12. 12 500 1p coins

PPM16
Addition and subtraction mix

1. 180 − 140 = 40
2.
   ```
     9 4 3
   − 2 4 0
   -------
     7 0 3
   ```
3. 729 + 89 = 818
4.
   ```
     2 3 4
   −   8 0
   -------
     1 5 4
   ```
5. 109 − 85 = 24
6.
   ```
     2 6 2
   + 2 2 1
   -------
     4 8 3
   ```
7. 418 − 9 = 409
8.
   ```
     5 6 7
   + 3 4 8
   -------
     9 1 5
   ```
9. 342 − 29 = 313
10.
    ```
      5 0 2
    − 4 7 9
    -------
        2 3
    ```
11. 557 + 41 = 598
12.
    ```
      5 1 0
    − 2 7 0
    -------
      2 4 0
    ```
13. 102 − 56 = 46
14.
    ```
      9 5 8
    + 7 7 5
    -------
    1 7 3 3
    ```
15. 452 + 123 = 575
16.
    ```
      8 2 6
    − 3 2 8
    -------
      4 9 8
    ```
17. 425 + 210 = 635
18.
    ```
      8 7 1
    + 7 9 7
    -------
    1 6 6 8
    ```
19. 431 + 289 = 720
20.
    ```
        5 8
    −   1 8
    -------
        4 0
    ```
21. 459 − 443 = 16

PPM17
Multiplication challenge

1. 52 × 7 = 350 + 14 = 364
2. 82 × 7 = 560 + 14 = 574
3. 93 × 5 = 450 + 15 = 465
4. 76 × 3 = 210 + 18 = 228
5. 35 × 2 = 60 + 10 = 70
6. 98 × 5 = 450 + 40 = 490
7. 58 × 2 = 100 + 16 = 116
8. 49 × 4 = 160 + 36 = 196
9. 78 × 3 = 210 + 24 = 234
10. 0 × 6 = 0
11. 32 × 7 = 210 + 14 = 224
12. 81 × 3 = 240 + 3 = 243
13. 19 × 6 = 60 + 54 = 114
14. 67 × 9 = 540 + 63 = 603
15. 94 × 4 = 360 +16 = 376
16. 21 × 6 = 120 + 6 = 126
17. 90 × 8 = 720 + 0 = 720
18. 43 × 3 = 120 + 9 = 129

PPM18
Digit values

1. 1473 → 4 hundreds
2. 274 → 4 units
3. 13 642 → 4 tens
4. 24 751 → 4 thousands
5. 43 073 → 40 thousands or 4 ten-thousands
6. 164 382 → 4 thousands
7. 3816 → 8 hundreds
8. 23 082 → 8 tens
9. 58 614 → 8 thousands
10. 84 329 → 80 thousands or 8 ten-thousands
11. 7628 → 8 units
12. 871 043 → 800 thousands or 8 hundred-thousands

PPM19
Temperature

1. 9 °C
2. -3 °C
3. -5 °C
4. -2 °C
5. 10 °C
6. -6 °C
7. -2 °C
8. -2 °C
9. -5 °C
10. -2 °C
11. 10 °C
12. 9 °C
13. -5 °C
14. 2 °C
15. -2 °C

PPM20
Positive and negative numbers

1. >, 2
2. <, 5
3. <, 10
4. >, 7
5. <, 2
6. <, 9
7. >, 8
8. <, 2
9. >, 4
10. >, 3
11. >, 6
12. <, 2
13. >, 10
14. >, 8
15. <, 5
16. <, 1
17. >, 1
18. <, 6
19. <, 1
20. >, 2

PPM21
Divisibility

1. 3 and 6
2. 3 and 9
3. 3 and 6 and 9
4. 3
5. 3 and 6
6. 3 and 6
7. 3
8. 3 and 6
9. 3 and 9
10. 2 and 4 and 8
11. 2 and 4 and 8
12. 2 and 4
13. 2 and 4 and 8
14. 2
15. 2 and 4
16. 2
17. 2 and 4 and 8
18. 2 and 4 and 8

PPM22
Tests for divisibility

1. True
2. False
3. True
4. True
5. False
6. True
7. True
8. True
9. False
10. True
11. 2: 96, 78, 372, 124, 56, 216, 192, 432, 175, 1044
12. 4: 96, 372, 124, 56, 216, 192, 432, 1044
13. 8: 96, 56, 216, 192, 432
14. 3: 96, 78, 372, 39, 216, 192, 432, 1044
15. 6: 96, 78, 372, 216, 192, 432, 1044
16. 9: 216, 432, 1044
17. 10: none
18. 25: 175
19. 50: none
20. 325 Yes
21. 175 Yes
22. 415 No
23. 865 No
24. 9000 Yes
25. 2775 Yes
26. 4320 No
27. 3025 Yes
28. 2750 Yes
29. 6155 No
30. 7080 No
31. 81 350 Yes

PPM23
Dividing by 10, 100 and 1000

1. 47 × 10 = 470
2. 850 ÷ 10 = 85
3. 7300 ÷ 10 = 730
4. 64 × 10 = 640
5. 9 × 100 = 900
6. 800 ÷ 100 = 8
7. 27 × 100 = 2700
8. 6300 ÷ 100 = 63
9. 83 × 10 = 830
10. 790 ÷ 10 = 79
11. 520 × 10 = 5200
12. 4320 ÷ 10 = 432
13. 18 × 100 = 1800
14. 1300 ÷ 100 = 13
15. 84 × 100 = 8400
16. 830 × 100 = 83 000
17. 46 × 100 = 4600
18. 700 ÷ 100 = 7
19. 160 × 100 = 16 000
20. 60 000 ÷ 100 = 600

PPM24
Units and digits of multiples

1	2	3	4	5	6	7	8	9	0
2	4	6	8	0	2	4	6	8	0
3	6	9	2	5	8	1	4	7	0
4	8	2	6	0	4	8	2	6	0
5	0	5	0	5	0	5	0	5	0
6	2	8	4	0	6	2	8	6	0
7	4	1	8	5	2	9	6	3	0
8	6	4	2	0	8	6	4	2	0
9	8	7	6	5	4	3	2	1	0
0	0	0	0	0	0	0	0	0	0

Answers will vary.

PPM25
Factors

1. 1, 2, 7, 14
2. 1, 2, 11, 22
3. 1, 2, 3, 4, 6, 8, 12, 24
4. 1, 2, 3, 5, 6, 10, 15, 30
5. 1, 2, 3, 4, 9, 12, 18, 36
6. 1, 2, 4, 11, 22, 44
7. 1, 3, 5, 9, 15, 45
8. 1, 2, 4, 7, 8, 14, 28, 56
9. False
10. True
11. False
12. True
13. True
14. False
15. True
16. 9
17. 6
18. 14
19. 9
20. 14
21. 7
22. 18

PPM26
Factors

1. 7 ← 8 → 11
2. 13 ← 14 → 17
3. 7 ← 10 → 11
4. 19 ← 20 → 23
5. 31 ← 35 → 37
6. 17 ← 18 → 19
7. 41 ← 42 → 43
8. 53 ← 54 → 59
9. 37 ← 38 → 41
10. 61 ← 62 → 67
11. 97 ← 98 → 101
12. 73 ← 76 → 79
13. 79 ← 82 → 83
14. 83 ← 88 → 89
15. 43 ← 44 → 47
16. 89 ← 95 → 97

PPM27
Factors

1. False: 'Five numbers have four factors.' In fact one number has four factors: 77.
   False: 'Only one number has six factors.' In fact two numbers have six factors: 75 (1, 3, 5, 15, 25, 75) and 76 (1, 2, 4, 19, 38, 76).
2. False: 'Only one number has three factors.' In fact none of these numbers have three factors.
   False: 'Only one number has eight factors,' In fact two numbers have eight factors: 70 (1, 2, 5, 7, 10, 14, 35, 70) and 78 (1, 2, 3, 6, 13, 26, 39, 78).

PPM28
Multiplying

Children's answers will vary.

PPM29
Order of operations

1. 6 − (12 ÷ 4) = 3
2. 7 + (1 × 6) = 13
3. (9 × 1) + 10 = 19

4. 12 − (5 × 2) = 2
5. (1 × 9) + 9 = 18
6. (8 × 10) − 7 = 73
7. 9 − (8 ÷ 8) = 8
8. 3 + (2 × 11) = 25
9. (12 ÷ 3) + 2 = 6
10. (4 × 4) − 3 = 13
11. 6 + (12 × 2) = 30
12. (4 × 5) − 4 = 16
13. (12 × 8) + 7 = 103
14. 12 + (3 × 5) = 27
15. 5 + (8 × 10) = 85
16. (10 ÷ 2) + 11 = 16
17. 7 − (1 × 3) = 4
18. 4 + (48 ÷ 8) = 10

PPM30
Order of operations

1. 43 + 10 − (2 × 10) = 43 + 10 − 20 = 33
2. (2 × 12) − 9 + 6 = 24 − 9 + 6 = 21
3. (3 × 11) − 9 + 2 = 33 − 9 + 2 = 26
4. 11 + (14 ÷ 7) + 1 = 11 + 2 + 1 = 14
5. (2 × 11) + 2 − 9 = 22 + 2 − 9 = 15
6. (2 × 8) − 3 − 2 = 16 − 3 − 2 = 11
7. (7 × 8) + (6 ÷ 3) = 56 + 2 = 58
8. (2 × 12) − (12 ÷ 4) = 24 − 3 = 21
9. 12 + (45 ÷ 9) − 11 = 12 + 5 − 11 = 6
10. 5 − (10 ÷ 2) − 8 = 5 − 5 − 8 = −8
11. (7 × 8) + (2 × 2) = 56 + 4 = 60
12. (3 ÷ 3) + (5 × 2) = 1 + 10 = 11
13. 5 + 2 + 11 + 2 = 20
14. 7 + 10 + (4 × 4) = 7 + 10 + 16 = 33
15. 7 + 7 − (2 × 5) = 14 − 10 = 4
16. 6 − (3 × 2) + 3 = 6 − 6 + 3 = 3
17. 12 + 11 + (7 × 6) = 12 + 11 + 42 = 65

PPM31
Rounding to the nearest thousand and hundred

1. 8000; 8400
2. 1000; 1100
3. 4000; 4400
4. 9000; 8900
5. 3000; 3500
6. 6000; 5600
7. 2000; 1900
8. 3000; 3300
9. 12 000; 11 500
10. 16 000; 16 400
11. 10 000; 9800
12. 4000; 4000

PPM32
Rounding to the nearest hundred

1. 3497 or 3479 → 3500
2. 4793 → 4800
3. 7349 → 7300
4. 9437 or 9374 → 9400
5. 4379 or 4397 → 4400
6. 3749 → 3700
7. 9347 → 9300
8. 7439 or 7394 → 7400
9. 7934 or 7943 → 7900
10. 4937 → 4900
11. 3794 → 3800
12. 9473 → 9500
13. 7493 → 7500
14. 3947 → 3900
15. 4973 → 5000
16. 9734 or 9743 → 9700

PPM33
Rounding in calculations

Calculation	Estimate with rounding both numbers	Actual answer of calculation	Difference between actual answer and estimate	Estimate with rounding the first number	Difference between actual answer and new estimate
82 + 36	80 + 40 = 120	118	2	80 + 36 = 116	2
38 + 44	40 + 40 = 80	82	2	40 + 44 = 84	2
67 + 24	70 + 20 = 90	91	1	70 + 24 = 94	3
78 + 14	80 + 10 = 90	92	2	80 + 14 = 94	2
38 + 52	40 + 50 = 90	90	0	40 + 52 = 92	2
65 + 74	70 + 70 = 140	139	1	70 + 74 = 144	5
16 + 84	20 + 80 = 100	100	0	20 + 84 = 104	4
96 + 46	100 + 50 = 150	142	8	100 + 46 = 146	4

PPM34
Rounding in calculations

Calculation	Estimate with rounding both numbers	Actual answer of calculation	Difference between actual answer and estimate	Estimate with rounding second number	Difference between actual answer and new estimate
74 − 16	70 − 20 = 50	58	8	74 − 20 = 54	4
96 − 59	100 − 60 = 40	37	3	96 − 60 = 36	1
98 − 19	100 − 20 = 80	79	1	98 − 20 = 78	1
73 − 15	70 − 20 = 50	58	8	73 − 20 = 53	5
48 − 19	50 − 20 = 30	29	1	48 − 20 = 28	1
64 − 48	60 − 50 = 10	16	6	64 − 50 = 14	2
73 − 25	70 − 30 = 40	48	8	73 − 30 = 43	5
92 − 44	90 − 40 = 50	48	2	92 − 40 = 52	4

PPM35
Arithmagons

1.
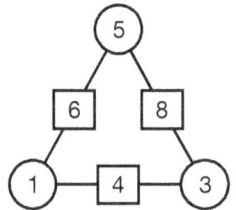

2.
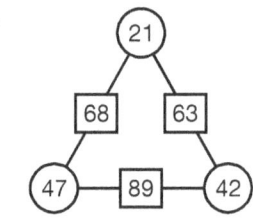

3.
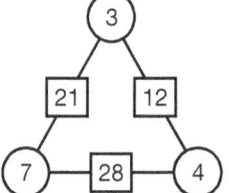

4.
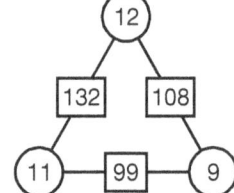

5.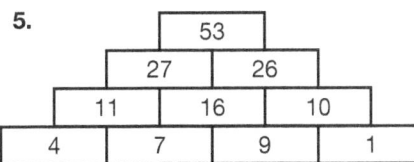

6.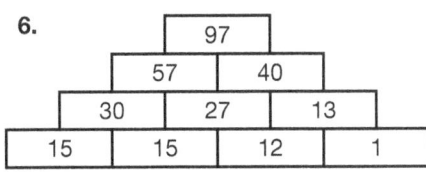

7.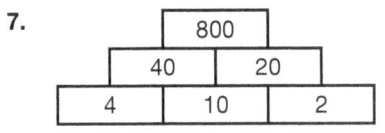

8.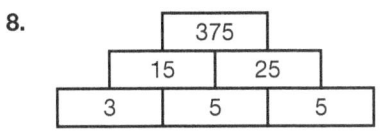

PPM36
Counting on and counting back

1. 48 + 24 = 72
2. 15 + 39 = 54
3. 87 + 58 = 145
4. 93 + 27 = 120
5. 63 + 27 = 90
6. 48 + 23 = 71
7. 73 + 25 = 98
8. Answers will vary.

PPM37
Making 1000

1. 700 + 300 = 1000
2. 600 + 400 = 1000
3. 250 + 750 = 1000
4. 350 + 650 = 1000
5. 675 + 325 = 1000
6. 296 + 704 = 1000
7. 310 + 690 = 1000
8. 320 + 680 = 1000
9. 5 + 995 = 1000
10. 530 + 470 = 1000
11. 190 + 810 = 1000
12. 750 + 250 = 1000
13. 50 + 950 = 1000
14. 280 + 720 = 1000
15. 140 + 860 = 1000
16. 150 + 850 = 1000
17. 730 + 270 = 1000
18. 640 + 360 = 1000
19. 550 + 450 = 1000
20. 325 + 675 = 1000

PPM38
Making the nearest 1000

1. 800 and 200
2. 660 and 340
3. 450 and 550
4. 150 and 850
5. 775 and 225
6. 295 and 705
7. 210 and 790
8. 920 and 80
9. 1180 and 820
10. 1550 and 450
11. 1150 and 850
12. 1380 and 620
13. 1160 and 840
14. 1050 and 950
15. 1630 and 370
16. 1250 and 750
17. 4280 and 720
18. 4310 and 690
19. 4620 and 380
20. 4290 and 710
21. 4505 and 495
22. 4895 and 105
23. 4550 and 450
24. 4940 and 60

PPM39
Near doubles

1. Double 72 = 144
2. 72 + 75 = 147
3. 68 + 72 = 140
4. 730 + 720 = 1450
5. Double 46 = 92
6. 49 + 46 = 95
7. 45 + 47 = 92
8. 460 + 480 = 940
9. Double 28 = 56
10. 28 + 29 = 57
11. 25 + 28 = 53
12. 260 + 280 = 540
13. Double 69 = 138
14. 72 + 69 = 141
15. 69 + 67 = 136
16. 680 + 670 = 1350
17. Double 57 = 114
18. 55 + 57 = 112
19. 57 + 59 = 116
20. 580 + 550 = 1130
21. Double 86 = 172
22. 86 + 89 = 175
23. 84 + 86 = 170
24. 870 + 860 = 1730

PPM40
Doubling

1.
94	166	56
134	148	68
182	112	106

2.
43	69	33
57	49	76
23	88	39

3.
148	52	178
238	134	276
116	314	86

PPM41
Doubles and halves

1. 340
2. 920
3. 520
4. 280
5. 230
6. 560
7. 740
8. 380
9. 880
10. 470
11. 160
12. 660
13. 970
14. 820
15. 70

PPM42
Rounding and multiplying

1. 29 × 4 = 116
2. 42 × 6 = 252
3. 48 × 8 = 384
4. 27 × 9 = 243

Answers will vary.

PPM43
Multiplying

Children's answers will vary.

PPM44
Multiplying

1. 7 × 30 = 210
2. 9 × 40 = 360
3. 4 × 60 = 240
4. 5 × 70 = 350
5. 70 × 7 = 490
6. 80 × 3 = 240
7. 90 × 7 = 630
8. 9 × 60 = 540
9. 7 × 400 = 2800
10. 500 × 4 = 2000
11. 8 × 800 = 6400
12. 6 × 800 = 4800
13. 9 × 3000 = 27 000
14. 8 × 90 = 720
15. 700 × 6 = 4200
16. 90 × 5 = 450
17. 3 × 600 = 1800
18. 6000 × 6 = 36 000
19. 3 × 6000 = 18 000
20. 8000 × 4 = 32 000

PPM45
Multiplying using grids

1. 6 × 20 =
   | | 10 | 10 |
   | 6 | 60 | 60 |

   6 × 20 = 120
2. 3 × 40 = 120
3. 4 × 50 = 200
4. 60 × 20 = 1200
5. 30 × 40 = 1200
6. 40 × 50 = 2000
7. Answers will vary.

PPM46
Multiplying by partitioning

1. $20 \times 60 = 2 \times 10 \times 6 \times 10$
   $= 2 \times 6 \times 10 \times 10$
   $= 12 \times 100$
   $= 1200$
2. $40 \times 30 = 1200$
3. $70 \times 80 = 5600$
4. $20 \times 30 \times 20 = 1200$
5. $10 \times 50 \times 30 = 15\,000$
6. $20 \times 30 \times 40 = 24\,000$
7. $10 \times 10 \times 20 \times 20 = 40\,000$
8. $20 \times 20 \times 20 \times 20 \times 20 \times 20 = 64\,000\,000$

PPM47
Multiplying

1.
   ```
        30   2
   7  [210][14]
   ```
   ```
     210
   +  14
     224
   ```
   $32 \times 7 = 224$

2.
   ```
        40   3
   8  [320][24]
   ```
   ```
     320
   +  24
     344
   ```
   $43 \times 8 = 344$

3.
   ```
        60   4
   9  [540][36]
   ```
   ```
     540
   +  36
     576
   ```
   $64 \times 9 = 576$

4.
   ```
        20   8
   4   [80][32]
   ```
   ```
      80
   +  32
     112
   ```
   $28 \times 4 = 112$

5.
   ```
        20   6
   6  [120][36]
   ```
   ```
     120
   +  36
     156
   ```
   $26 \times 6 = 156$

6.
   ```
        30   5
   9  [270][45]
   ```
   ```
     270
   +  45
     315
   ```
   $35 \times 9 = 315$

7.
   ```
        50   9
   7  [350][63]
   ```
   ```
     350
   +  63
     413
   ```
   $59 \times 7 = 413$

8.
   ```
        80   7
   5  [400][35]
   ```
   ```
     400
   +  35
     435
   ```
   $87 \times 5 = 435$

PPM48
Multiplying

1. 432×6
   ```
         400   30   2
   6  [2400][180][12]
   ```
   ```
       2400
        180
   +     12
       2592
   ```
   $432 \times 6 = 2592$

2. $144 \times 8 = 1152$
3. $215 \times 9 = 1935$
4. $670 \times 5 = 3350$
5. $329 \times 7 = 2303$
6. $508 \times 4 = 2032$

PPM49
Multiplying

1.
   ```
      (90)
       17
   ×    3
       51
   ```
2. 222
3. 172
4. 512
5. 280
6. 760
7. 468
8. 427
9. 462

Answers will vary.

PPM50
Multiplying

1.
   ```
      (60)
       24
   ×    3
       72
   ```
2. 152
3. 413
4. 340
5. 424
6. 282
7. 384
8. 315
9. 243

PPM51
Multiplying

Children's answers will vary.

PPM52
Multiplying

Children will write their estimates in the empty ovals.

1.
   ```
      126
   ×    4
      504
       12
   ```

2.
   ```
      217
   ×    3
      651
        2
   ```

3.
   ```
      342
   ×    5
     1710
       21
   ```

4.
   ```
      434
   ×    6
     2604
       22
   ```

5.
   ```
      573
   ×    3
     1719
        2
   ```

6.
   ```
      289
   ×    4
     1156
       33
   ```

7.
   ```
      717
   ×    5
     3585
        3
   ```

8.
   ```
      386
   ×    7
     2702
       64
   ```

9.
   ```
      294
   ×    3
      882
       21
   ```

PPM53
Multiplying

Children will write their estimates in the empty ovals. Their answers will vary.

PPM54
Multiplying

Children will write their estimates in the empty ovals. Their answers will vary.

PPM55
Who is right?

It doesn't matter which grid the boys draw. But Lewis made 6×9 to be 48 instead of 54. His answer is wrong and Fraser's is right.

PPM56
Multiplying

Children will write their estimations in the empty ovals.

1.
   ```
        27
   ×    18
       216
        5
   +   270
       486
   ```

2. $42 \times 16 = 672$
3. $35 \times 17 = 595$
4. $35 \times 22 = 770$
5. $46 \times 27 = 1242$
6. $64 \times 23 = 1472$
7. $54 \times 33 = 1782$
8. $47 \times 34 = 1598$
9. $56 \times 38 = 2128$

PPM57

Multiplication using the grid method

1. 13 × 45

	40	5
10	10 × 40 = 400	10 × 5 = 50
3	3 × 40 = 120	3 × 5 = 15

```
  4 5 0
+ 1 3 5
-------
  5 8 5
```

2. 86 × 38

	30	8
80	80 × 30 = 2400	80 × 8 = 640
6	6 × 30 = 180	6 × 8 = 48

```
  3 0 4 0
+   2 2 8
---------
  3 2 6 8
```

3. 58 × 37

	30	7
50	50 × 30 = 1500	50 × 7 = 350
8	8 × 30 = 240	8 × 7 = 56

```
  1 8 5 0
+   2 9 6
---------
  2 1 4 6
```

4. 69 × 24

	60	9
20	60 × 20 = 1200	9 × 20 = 180
4	60 × 40 = 240	9 × 4 = 36

```
  1 3 8 0
+   2 7 6
---------
  1 6 5 6
```

5. Children's answers will vary.

PPM58

More multiplication by the grid method

1. 531 × 27

	500	30	1
20	500 × 20 = 10 000	30 × 20 = 600	1 × 20 = 20
7	500 × 7 = 3500	30 × 7 = 210	1 × 7 = 7

```
  1 0 6 2 0
+   3 7 1 7
-----------
  1 4 3 3 7
```

2. 358 × 27

	300	50	8
20	300 × 20 = 6000	50 × 20 = 1000	8 × 20 = 160
7	300 × 7 = 2100	50 × 7 = 350	8 × 7 = 56

```
  7 1 6 0
+ 2 5 0 6
---------
  9 6 6 6
```

3. 469 × 68

	400	60	9
60	400 × 60 = 24 000	60 × 60 = 3600	9 × 60 = 540
8	400 × 8 = 3200	60 × 8 = 480	9 × 8 = 72

```
  2 8 1 4 0
+   3 7 5 2
-----------
  3 1 8 9 2
```

4. 509 × 62

	500	0	9
60	500 × 60 = 30 000	0 × 60 = 0	9 × 60 = 540
2	500 × 2 = 1000	0 × 2 = 0	9 × 2 = 18

```
  3 0 5 4 0
+   1 0 1 8
-----------
  3 1 5 5 8
```

5. Children's answers will vary.

PPM59

Multiplying

1.
```
    1 3 6
  ×   2 4
  -------
    5 4 4
      1 2
+ 2 7 2 0
      1
---------
  3 2 6 4
```

2. 249 × 18 = 4482
3. 306 × 32 = 9792
4. 417 × 16 = 6672
5. 532 × 23 = 12 236
6. 618 × 31 = 19 158
7. 279 × 27 = 7533
8. 384 × 36 = 13 824
9. 526 × 44 = 23 144

PPM60

More multiplying

Children's answers will vary.

PPM61
Stepping backwards

Size of step		Where I land	Number of steps	Division calculation
18	3	15 12 9 6 3 0	6	18 ÷ 3 = 6
42	6	36 30 24 18 12 6 0	7	42 ÷ 6 = 7
20	4	16 12 8 4 0	5	20 ÷ 4 = 5
32	8	24 16 8 0	4	32 ÷ 8 = 4
12	3	9 6 3 0	4	12 ÷ 3 = 4
54	9	45 36 27 18 9 0	6	54 ÷ 9 = 6
35	5	30 25 20 15 10 5 0	7	35 ÷ 5 = 7
44	11	33 22 11 0	4	44 ÷ 11 = 4
27	9	18 9 0	3	27 ÷ 9 = 3
45	9	36 27 18 9 0	5	45 ÷ 9 = 4
40	8	32 24 16 8 0	5	40 ÷ 8 = 5
24	8	16 8 0	3	24 ÷ 8 = 3

PPM62
Stepping backwards

Size of step		Where I land	Number of steps	Division calculation
20	3	17 14 11 8 5 2	6	20 ÷ 3 = 6 r 2
45	6	39 33 27 21 15 9 3	7	45 ÷ 6 = 7 r 3
23	4	19 15 11 7 3	5	23 ÷ 4 = 5 r 3
36	8	28 20 12 4	4	36 ÷ 8 = 4 r 4
14	3	11 8 5 2	4	14 ÷ 3 = 4 r 2
57	9	48 39 30 21 12 3	6	57 ÷ 9 = 6 r 3
39	5	34 29 24 19 14 9 4	7	39 ÷ 5 = 7 r 4
49	11	38 27 16 5	4	49 ÷ 11 = 4 r 5
31	9	22 13 4	3	31 ÷ 9 = 3 r 4
48	9	39 30 21 12 3	5	48 ÷ 9 = 5 r 3
43	8	35 27 19 11 3	5	43 ÷ 8 = 5 r 3
26	8	18 10 2	3	26 ÷ 8 = 3 r 2

PPM63
Chunking in 5s

1. 76 ÷ 5
   ```
       7 6
   -  5 0   (10) × 5
       2 6
   -  2 5   (5) × 5
       1      = 15 r 1
   ```
2. 83 ÷ 5 = 16 r 3
3. 97 ÷ 5 = 19 r 2
4. 85 ÷ 5 = 17
5. 68 ÷ 5 = 13 r 3
6. 72 ÷ 5 = 14 r 2

Answers will vary.

PPM64
Chunking

1. 81 ÷ 7
   ```
       8 1
   -  7 0   (10) × 7
       2 1
   -  2 1   (3) × 7
       0      = 13
   ```
2. 54 ÷ 8 = 6 r 6
3. 73 ÷ 6 = 12 r 1
4. 69 ÷ 4 = 17 r 1
5. 94 ÷ 3 = 31 r 1
6. 82 ÷ 4 = 20 r 2

Answers will vary.

PPM65
Dividing

1. ```
       1 4
   3)4 2
       3 0   (10) × 3
       1 2   (4) × 3
       0
   ```
2. ```
       1 3
   3)3 9
       3 0   (10) × 3
       9     (3) × 3
       0
   ```
3. ```
       1 8
   4)7 2
       4 0   (10) × 4
       3 2   (8) × 4
       0
   ```
4. ```
       1 7
   5)8 5
       5 0   (10) × 5
       3 5   (7) × 5
       0
   ```
5. ```
       1 6
   6)9 6
       6 0   (10) × 6
       3 6   (6) × 6
       0
   ```
6. ```
       1 6
   3)4 8
       3 0   (10) × 3
       1 8   (6) × 3
       0
   ```
7. ```
       1 3
   7)9 1
       7 0   (10) × 7
       2 1   (3) × 7
       0
   ```
8. ```
       1 4
   4)5 6
       4 0   (10) × 4
       1 6   (4) × 4
       0
   ```
9. ```
       1 4
   6)8 4
       6 0   (10) × 6
       2 4   (4) × 6
       0
   ```

PPM66
Dividing 3-digit numbers

Children's choice as to the 'chunks' to subtract may vary.

1. 438 ÷ 5 = 87 r 3
2. 782 ÷ 8 = 97 r 6
3. 303 ÷ 8 = 37 r 7
4. 472 ÷ 3 = 157 r 1
5. 781 ÷ 6 = 130 r 1
   ```

PPM67
Dividing by multiples of 10

1.
```
        4 0
   20)8 0 0
      2 0 0   (10) × 20
      ─────
      6 0 0
      2 0 0   (10) × 20
      ─────
      4 0 0
      2 0 0   (10) × 20
      ─────
      2 0 0
      2 0 0   (10) × 20
      ─────
          0
```
800 ÷ 20 = 40
Children's choice as to the 'chunks' to subtract may vary.

2. 600 ÷ 30 = 20
3. 900 ÷ 20 = 45
4. 780 ÷ 20 = 39
5. 920 ÷ 40 = 23

PPM68
Dividing by multiples of 10 again

1.
```
        4 0 r 3
   20)4 6 3
      2 0 0   (10) × 20
      ─────
      2 6 3
      2 0 0   (10) × 20
      ─────
        6 3
        6 0   (3) × 20
      ─────
          0
```
463 ÷ 20 = 23 r 3
Children's choice as to the 'chunks' to subtract may vary.

2. 638 ÷ 30 = 21 r 8
3. 889 ÷ 40 = 22 r 9
4. 973 ÷ 50 = 19 r 23
5. 918 ÷ 40 = 22 r 38

PPM69
Dividing 2-digit numbers

1. 40 ÷ 5 = 8
2. 28 ÷ 7 = 4
3. 36 ÷ 6 = 6
4. 85 ÷ 5 = 17
5. 64 ÷ 4 = 16
6. 78 ÷ 6 = 13
7. 96 ÷ 8 = 12
8. 84 ÷ 7 = 12
9. 94 ÷ 6 = 15 r 4
10. 72 ÷ 4 = 18
11. 52 ÷ 2 = 26
12. 73 ÷ 3 = 24 r 1
13. 72 ÷ 3 = 24
14. 91 ÷ 7 = 13
15. 72 ÷ 6 = 12
16. 68 ÷ 4 = 17
17. 99 ÷ 9 = 11
18. 84 ÷ 7 = 12
19. 96 ÷ 4 = 24
20. 65 ÷ 5 = 13
21. 87 ÷ 3 = 29
22. 46 ÷ 2 = 23
23. 75 ÷ 5 = 15
24. 98 ÷ 7 = 14

PPM70
Dividing 3-digit numbers

1. 413 ÷ 5 = 82 r 3
2. 281 ÷ 7 = 40 r 1
3. 375 ÷ 6 = 62 r 3
4. 892 ÷ 5 = 178 r 2
5. 291 ÷ 4 = 72 r 3
6. 423 ÷ 6 = 70 r 3
7. 242 ÷ 8 = 30 r 2
8. 876 ÷ 7 = 125 r 1
9. 191 ÷ 6 = 31 r 5
10. 824 ÷ 8 = 103
11. 515 ÷ 2 = 257 r 1
12. 707 ÷ 3 = 235 r 2
13. 721 ÷ 3 = 240 r 1
14. 829 ÷ 7 = 118 r 3
15. 923 ÷ 6 = 153 r 5
16. 676 ÷ 4 = 169
17. 778 ÷ 9 = 88 r 4
18. 461 ÷ 7 = 65 r 6
19. 974 ÷ 4 = 243 r 2
20. 620 ÷ 5 = 124
21. 927 ÷ 5 = 185 r 2
22. 863 ÷ 7 = 123 r 2
23. 715 ÷ 4 = 178 r 3
24. 850 ÷ 7 = 121 r 3

PPM71
Word problems

1. 822 points
2. 88 points
3. 1041 points
4. 165 points

Answers 3 and 4 should be circled.

5. Answers will vary.
6. 330 + 188 = 518
7. 522 × 4 = 2088
8. 435 − 276 = 159
9. 268 ÷ 4 = 67

PPM72
Word problems
Children's answers will vary.

PPM73
Thinking it through 1
Children's answers will vary.

PPM74
Thinking it through 2
Children's answers will vary.

PPM75
Thinking it through 3
Children's answers will vary.

Whole Number APMs

APM 180
Eratosthenes' sieve

1. 1, 2, 3, 5, 7, 11, 13, 17, 19, 23, 29, 31, 37, 41, 43, 47, 53, 59, 61, 67, 71, 73, 79, 83, 89, 97
2. They are prime numbers. Each number is only divisible by itself and 1.
3. Multiples of 4 and 8 are also multiples of 2.
   Multiples of 6 and 9 are also multiples of 3.

APM 183
100-square questions

23 × 34 = 782
24 × 33 = 792, which is 10 more.
Children will find that this applies to any 2 by 2 square. The calculation with the top-left and bottom-right number will be 10 less than the calculation with the top-right and bottom-left numbers.
23 × 45 = 1035
25 × 43 = 1075, which is 40 more.
Children will find that this applies to any 3 by 3 square. The calculation with the top-left and bottom-right numbers will be 40 less than the calculation with the top-right and bottom-left numbers.
The difference between the calculations increases with the size of the square.

Square	Difference	Difference increase
2 by 2 square	10	–
3 by 3 square	40	30
4 by 4 square	90	50
5 by 5 square	160	70
6 by 6 square	250	90

Children may find a pattern in the differences and also in the difference increase each time. Some children may be able to relate the differences pattern to square numbers. Children may relate the difference increase pattern to the odd number 2 times-table; 3, 5, 7, 9, … . Able children may be able to use the equation $d = 10(n - 1)^2$ to find any difference, where d = the difference between the two calculations and n = the dimension of the square.
These patterns apply no matter what the start and end numbers of the squares are.

APM 184
I know … so I know …

Children will notice that when they write multiplication calculations using as many numbers as possible, each of the

numbers used will be a prime number. They are called prime factors.
For example, 300 = 2 × 2 × 5 × 3 × 5, so the prime factors of 300 are 2, 3 and 5.
1500 = 3 × 5 × 2 × 5 × 2 × 5, so the prime factors of 1500 are 2, 3 and 5. Children may notice that any numbers which are common multiples, such as 300 and 1500, will also have the same prime factors.

APM 185
Line multiplication

The diagrams show that you are:
multiplying the tens of one number by the tens of the other number
and
multiplying the tens of one number by the units of the other number
and
multiplying the units of one number by the tens of the other number
and
multiplying the units of one number by the units of the other number.

Fractions, Decimals and Percentages, Pupil Book 2

Page 3
Mixed numbers and improper fractions

1. $2\frac{1}{4}$ 2. $1\frac{3}{4}$ 3. $3\frac{1}{2}$
4. $1\frac{2}{3}$ 5. $2\frac{1}{3}$ 6. $3\frac{2}{3}$
7. $1\frac{3}{8}$ 8. $2\frac{1}{8}$ 9. $3\frac{7}{8}$

Rocket
1. $2\frac{3}{4}$ 2. $3\frac{1}{4}$ 3. $1\frac{1}{2}$
4. $3\frac{1}{3}$ 5. $2\frac{2}{3}$ 6. $1\frac{1}{3}$
7. $3\frac{5}{8}$ 8. $2\frac{7}{8}$ 9. $1\frac{1}{8}$
10. $1\frac{1}{4} = \frac{5}{4}$ 11. $2\frac{3}{4} = \frac{11}{4}$
12. $3\frac{1}{4} = \frac{13}{4}$ 13. $5 = \frac{20}{4}$
14. $1\frac{2}{3} = \frac{5}{3}$ 15. $3\frac{1}{3} = \frac{10}{3}$
16. $5\frac{2}{3} = \frac{17}{3}$ 17. $3 = \frac{9}{3}$
18. $1\frac{3}{5} = \frac{8}{5}$ 19. $2\frac{1}{5} = \frac{11}{5}$
20. $3\frac{4}{5} = \frac{19}{5}$ 21. $6\frac{3}{5} = \frac{33}{5}$

Page 4
Mixed numbers and improper fractions

1. $2\frac{5}{6}$ 2. $3\frac{3}{4}$ 3. $2\frac{1}{3}$
4. $4\frac{5}{8}$ 5. $3\frac{3}{5}$ 6. $1\frac{7}{10}$
7. $1\frac{8}{9}$ 8. $5\frac{1}{2}$ 9. $3\frac{7}{12}$
10. 7   11. 10   12. 17
13. 17   14. 7   15. 30
16. 34   17. 23   18. 27
19. 13   20. 31   21. 27
22. 7   23. 11   24. 23

Rocket 100 minutes = $1\frac{40}{60}$ or $1\frac{2}{3}$ hours;
150 minutes = $2\frac{30}{60}$ or $2\frac{1}{2}$ hours;
200 minutes = $3\frac{20}{60}$ or $3\frac{1}{3}$ hours;
10 days = $1\frac{3}{7}$ weeks;
20 days = $2\frac{6}{7}$ weeks;
30 days = $4\frac{2}{7}$ weeks.

Page 5
Mixed numbers and improper fractions

1. $1\frac{1}{2}$ 2. $1\frac{1}{3}$
3. $1\frac{3}{4}$ 4. $1\frac{3}{10}$
5. $2\frac{3}{5}$ 6. $2\frac{5}{8}$
7. $2\frac{3}{7}$ 8. $8\frac{2}{6}$ or $8\frac{1}{3}$

Rocket Children should be able to make more than ten different improper fractions.

9. $2\frac{3}{5}$ 10. $2\frac{1}{4}$
11. $4\frac{2}{7}$ 12. $2\frac{5}{6}$
13. $6\frac{1}{2}$ 14. $1\frac{3}{10}$
15. $3\frac{7}{8}$

Page 6
Mixed numbers and improper fractions

1. $\frac{13}{3}$ 2. $\frac{27}{5}$ 3. $\frac{7}{4}$
4. $\frac{34}{5}$ 5. $\frac{23}{8}$ 6. $\frac{17}{10}$
7. $\frac{26}{7}$ 8. $\frac{11}{6}$ 9. $\frac{35}{8}$
10. $\frac{35}{3}$ 11. $\frac{57}{4}$ 12. $\frac{77}{9}$
13. $\frac{44}{12}$ 14. $\frac{82}{11}$ 15. $\frac{113}{9}$
16. $\frac{103}{15}$

Rocket Answers will vary. The highest mixed number is $4\frac{1}{2}$ and the lowest is $1\frac{1}{9}$.

17. 8   18. 4   19. 11
20. 4   21. 6   22. 4
23. 87   24. 5   25. 4
26. 39   27. 2   28. 3

Page 7
Mixed numbers and improper fractions

1. $3\frac{1}{2} < \frac{9}{2}$ 2. $4\frac{2}{3} < \frac{16}{3}$
3. $\frac{27}{4} > 5\frac{3}{4}$ 4. $\frac{21}{5} > 3\frac{4}{5}$
5. $3\frac{7}{10} > \frac{31}{10}$ 6. $\frac{23}{6} = 3\frac{5}{6}$
7. $\frac{38}{7} > 5\frac{2}{7}$ 8. $\frac{59}{9} < 6\frac{7}{9}$
9. $4\frac{3}{8} > \frac{31}{8}$ 10. $2\frac{5}{12} = \frac{29}{12}$
11. $1\frac{3}{4}, 2\frac{1}{3}, 2\frac{1}{2}, 4\frac{1}{5}, 5\frac{3}{10}$
12. $2\frac{7}{10}, 3\frac{5}{6}, 4\frac{5}{8}, 5\frac{1}{3}, 6\frac{3}{4}$
13. $\frac{8}{9}, 1\frac{3}{7}, 2\frac{4}{5}, 3\frac{5}{8}, 4\frac{2}{3}$
14. $1\frac{5}{8}, 4\frac{2}{9}, 5\frac{3}{4}, 6\frac{3}{6}, 8\frac{1}{4}$
15. $2\frac{3}{4}, 3\frac{5}{8}, 4\frac{1}{2}, 5\frac{5}{6}, 7\frac{2}{3}$
16. $1\frac{7}{10}, 2\frac{4}{7}, 4\frac{5}{8}, 7\frac{1}{4}, 8\frac{2}{3}$

Rocket Answers will vary.

17. $\frac{3}{4}$ 18. $\frac{3}{6}$
19. $\frac{5}{2}$ 20. $\frac{7}{3}$

Page 8
Equivalent fractions

Shaded fractions:
1. $\frac{1}{2} = \frac{2}{4}$ 2. $\frac{1}{3} = \frac{2}{6}$
3. $\frac{4}{10} = \frac{2}{5}$ 4. $\frac{1}{4} = \frac{2}{8}$
5. $\frac{1}{2} = \frac{3}{6}$ 6. $\frac{6}{8} = \frac{3}{4}$
7. $\frac{4}{6} = \frac{2}{3}$ 8. $\frac{1}{3} = \frac{3}{9}$

Unshaded fractions:
1. $\frac{1}{2} = \frac{2}{4}$ 2. $\frac{2}{3} = \frac{4}{6}$
3. $\frac{6}{10} = \frac{3}{5}$ 4. $\frac{3}{4} = \frac{6}{8}$
5. $\frac{1}{2} = \frac{3}{6}$ 6. $\frac{2}{8} = \frac{1}{4}$
7. $\frac{2}{6} = \frac{1}{3}$ 8. $\frac{2}{3} = \frac{6}{9}$

Rocket Answers will vary.

Page 9
Equivalent fractions

1. a, g: $\frac{4}{8} = \frac{1}{2}$
   b, e: $\frac{1}{3} = \frac{2}{6}$
   c, f: $\frac{1}{4} = \frac{2}{8}$
   d, k: $\frac{3}{4} = \frac{6}{8}$
   h, l: $\frac{3}{5} = \frac{6}{10}$
   i, j: $\frac{4}{6} = \frac{2}{3}$

2. Answers will vary.

Rocket Answers will vary.

$\frac{1}{4} = \frac{2}{8}$
$\frac{1}{3} = \frac{2}{6}$
$\frac{1}{2} = \frac{2}{4} = \frac{3}{6} = \frac{4}{8}$
$\frac{2}{3} = \frac{4}{6}$
$\frac{3}{4} = \frac{6}{8}$

If you add cards 9 and 10:
$\frac{1}{3} = \frac{2}{6} = \frac{3}{9}$
$\frac{1}{2} = \frac{2}{4} = \frac{3}{6} = \frac{4}{8} = \frac{5}{10}$
$\frac{2}{3} = \frac{4}{6} = \frac{6}{9}$
$\frac{1}{5} = \frac{2}{10}$
$\frac{2}{5} = \frac{4}{10}$
$\frac{3}{5} = \frac{6}{10}$
$\frac{4}{5} = \frac{8}{10}$

Page 10
Equivalent fractions

1. $\frac{1}{2} = \frac{2}{4}$ 2. $\frac{2}{4} = \frac{4}{8}$
3. $\frac{2}{2} = \frac{4}{4}$ 4. $\frac{6}{8} = \frac{3}{4}$
5. $\frac{1}{2} = \frac{4}{8}$ 6. $1 = \frac{4}{4}$
7. $\frac{1}{3} = \frac{2}{6}$ 8. $\frac{2}{4} = \frac{4}{6}$
9. $\frac{3}{6} = \frac{6}{12}$ 10. $\frac{2}{3} = \frac{8}{12}$
11. $\frac{1}{3} = \frac{4}{12}$ 12. $\frac{3}{3} = \frac{6}{6}$

Rocket

1				
$\frac{1}{5}$	$\frac{1}{5}$	$\frac{1}{5}$	$\frac{1}{5}$	$\frac{1}{5}$
$\frac{1}{10}$ $\frac{1}{10}$	$\frac{1}{10}$ $\frac{1}{10}$	$\frac{1}{10}$ $\frac{1}{10}$	$\frac{1}{10}$ $\frac{1}{10}$	$\frac{1}{10}$ $\frac{1}{10}$
$\frac{1}{20}$ $\frac{1}{20}$ $\frac{1}{20}$ $\frac{1}{20}$	$\frac{1}{20}$ $\frac{1}{20}$ $\frac{1}{20}$ $\frac{1}{20}$	$\frac{1}{20}$ $\frac{1}{20}$ $\frac{1}{20}$ $\frac{1}{20}$	$\frac{1}{20}$ $\frac{1}{20}$ $\frac{1}{20}$ $\frac{1}{20}$	$\frac{1}{20}$ $\frac{1}{20}$ $\frac{1}{20}$ $\frac{1}{20}$

13. 4
14. $\frac{2}{6}$ or $\frac{1}{3}$. 10 children
15. $\frac{2}{6}$ or $\frac{1}{3}$

Page 11
Equivalent fractions
1. $\frac{1}{2}, \frac{2}{4}, \frac{4}{8}$
2. $\frac{2}{3}, \frac{4}{6}, \frac{8}{12}$
3. $\frac{3}{4}, \frac{6}{8}, \frac{12}{16}$
4. $\frac{1}{2}, \frac{4}{8}, \frac{8}{16}$
5. $\frac{3}{5}, \frac{6}{10}, \frac{12}{20}$
6. $\frac{60}{100} = \frac{6}{10}$
7. $\frac{1}{2} = \frac{5}{10}$
8. $\frac{1}{2} = \frac{50}{100}$
9. $\frac{10}{100} = \frac{1}{10}$
10. $\frac{9}{10} = \frac{90}{100}$
11. $\frac{1}{4} = \frac{25}{100}$
12. $\frac{3}{4} = \frac{75}{100}$
13. $\frac{4}{10} = \frac{40}{100}$

Rocket Answers will vary.

Page 12
Equivalent fractions
1. $\frac{1}{4} = \frac{2}{8}$
2. $\frac{1}{2} = \frac{2}{4}$
3. $\frac{4}{8} = \frac{2}{4}$
4. $\frac{3}{4} = \frac{6}{8}$
5. $\frac{1}{2} = \frac{4}{8}$
6. $\frac{1}{3} = \frac{2}{6}$
7. $\frac{3}{6} = \frac{6}{12}$
8. $\frac{1}{6} = \frac{2}{12}$
9. $\frac{2}{3} = \frac{8}{12}$
10. $\frac{4}{6} = \frac{2}{3}$
11. $\frac{5}{6} = \frac{10}{12}$

Rocket Answers will vary.

12. A and G
    B and N
    C and I
    D and K
    E and J
    F and M
    H and L
13. Answers will vary.

Page 13
Fractions in their simplest form
1. 1, 2, 4, 5, 10, 20
2. 1, 2, 3, 5, 6, 10, 15, 30
3. 1, 2, 4, 8, 16
4. 1, 2, 4, 7, 14, 28
5. 1, 2, 3, 4, 6, 12
6. 1, 2, 4, 8
7. 1, 2, 3, 6, 9, 18
8. 1, 2, 4, 8, 16, 32
9. 1, 5, 25
10. 1, 2, 3, 4, 6, 9, 12, 18, 36
11. 1, 2, 3, 4, 6, 8, 12, 24
12. 1, 2, 4, 5, 8, 10, 20, 40
13. $\frac{2}{4} = \frac{1}{2}$
14. $\frac{2}{8} = \frac{1}{4}$
15. $\frac{6}{9} = \frac{2}{3}$
16. $\frac{3}{12} = \frac{1}{4}$
17. $\frac{2}{10} = \frac{1}{5}$
18. $\frac{10}{15} = \frac{2}{3}$
19. $\frac{6}{8} = \frac{3}{4}$
20. $\frac{12}{20} = \frac{3}{5}$
21. $\frac{8}{12} = \frac{2}{3}$
22. $\frac{12}{30} = \frac{2}{5}$
23. $\frac{32}{40} = \frac{4}{5}$
24. $\frac{6}{36} = \frac{1}{6}$

Rocket Answers will vary.

Page 14
Fractions in their simplest form
1. $\frac{9}{12} = \frac{3}{4}$
2. $\frac{8}{10} = \frac{4}{5}$
3. $\frac{6}{9} = \frac{2}{3}$
4. $\frac{12}{18} = \frac{2}{3}$
5. $\frac{15}{40} = \frac{3}{8}$
6. $\frac{20}{24} = \frac{5}{6}$
7. $\frac{18}{30} = \frac{3}{5}$
8. $\frac{21}{28} = \frac{3}{4}$
9. $\frac{14}{42} = \frac{1}{3}$
10. $\frac{36}{100} = \frac{9}{25}$
11. $\frac{24}{50} = \frac{12}{25}$
12. $\frac{49}{63} = \frac{7}{9}$
13. $\frac{3}{5} = \frac{6}{10}$
14. $\frac{4}{7} = \frac{12}{21}$
15. $\frac{5}{9} = \frac{20}{36}$
16. $\frac{2}{3} = \frac{16}{24}$
17. $\frac{15}{40} = \frac{3}{8}$
18. $\frac{35}{42} = \frac{5}{6}$
19. $\frac{1}{9} = \frac{8}{72}$
20. $\frac{7}{5} = \frac{28}{20}$
21. $\frac{4}{3} = \frac{28}{21}$
22. $\frac{21}{28} = \frac{3}{4}$
23. $\frac{25}{45} = \frac{5}{9}$
24. $\frac{7}{8} = \frac{42}{48}$

Rocket Answers will vary.

Page 15
Fractions in their simplest form
1. $\frac{1}{2}$
2. $\frac{1}{4}$
3. $\frac{1}{2}$
4. $\frac{2}{3}$
5. $\frac{3}{5}$
6. $\frac{2}{3}$
7. $\frac{2}{3}$
8. $\frac{4}{5}$

9–12. Answers will vary.

Rocket $\frac{60}{80} = \frac{3}{4}$
Answers will vary for the number of steps children take.
$\frac{72}{80} = \frac{9}{10}$
Answers will vary for children's own fraction problems.

Page 16
Fractions in their simplest form
1. $\frac{9}{6} = \frac{3}{2} = 1\frac{1}{2}$
2. $\frac{14}{10} = \frac{7}{5} = 1\frac{2}{5}$
3. $\frac{18}{4} = \frac{9}{2} = 4\frac{1}{2}$
4. $\frac{34}{8} = \frac{17}{4} = 4\frac{1}{4}$
5. $\frac{26}{8} = \frac{13}{4} = 3\frac{1}{4}$
6. $\frac{14}{10} = \frac{7}{5} = 1\frac{2}{5}$
7. $\frac{42}{4} = \frac{21}{2} = 10\frac{1}{2}$
8. $\frac{40}{6} = \frac{20}{3} = 6\frac{2}{3}$
9. $\frac{18}{8} \neq \frac{21}{4}$
10. $\frac{32}{3} = \frac{96}{9}$
11. $\frac{26}{7} = \frac{104}{28}$
12. $\frac{24}{5} \neq \frac{26}{10}$
13. $\frac{22}{5} = \frac{66}{15}$
14. $\frac{45}{12} \neq \frac{25}{6}$
15. Answers will vary.

Rocket Answers will vary.

Page 17
Ordering fractions
1. $\frac{1}{3}, \frac{3}{4}$
2. $\frac{3}{5}, \frac{2}{3}$
3. $\frac{1}{4}, \frac{2}{5}$
4. $\frac{1}{2}, \frac{5}{6}$
5. $\frac{2}{5}, \frac{5}{8}$
6. $\frac{4}{5}, \frac{7}{8}$
7. $\frac{1}{3}, \frac{1}{2}, \frac{2}{3}$
8. $\frac{1}{4}, \frac{2}{3}, \frac{3}{5}$
9. $\frac{2}{5}, \frac{2}{4}$ (or $\frac{1}{2}$), $\frac{4}{5}$
10. $\frac{1}{5}, \frac{2}{6}, \frac{5}{6}$

Rocket Answers will vary but may include the following:
7. $\frac{1}{3}, \frac{1}{2}, \frac{2}{3} = \frac{2}{6}, \frac{3}{6}, \frac{4}{6}$
8. $\frac{1}{4}, \frac{2}{3}, \frac{3}{4} = \frac{3}{12}, \frac{8}{12}, \frac{9}{12}$
9. $\frac{2}{5}, \frac{1}{2}, \frac{4}{5} = \frac{4}{10}, \frac{5}{10}, \frac{8}{10}$
10. $\frac{1}{5}, \frac{2}{6}, \frac{5}{6} = \frac{6}{30}, \frac{10}{30}, \frac{25}{30}$

Page 18
Ordering fractions
1. a: $\frac{6}{12} = \frac{1}{2}$
   b: $\frac{3}{12} = \frac{1}{4}$
   c: $\frac{10}{12} = \frac{5}{6}$
   d: $\frac{4}{12} = \frac{1}{3}$
   e: $\frac{8}{12} = \frac{2}{3}$
   f: $\frac{9}{12} = \frac{3}{4}$
   g: $\frac{11}{12}$
   h: $\frac{1}{12}$
2. $\frac{5}{12} > \frac{1}{2}$
3. $\frac{6}{15} > \frac{1}{3}$
4. $\frac{4}{5} < \frac{18}{20}$
5. $\frac{1}{2} > \frac{7}{16}$
6. $\frac{3}{8} > \frac{1}{4}$
7. $\frac{7}{15} > \frac{13}{30}$

8–15.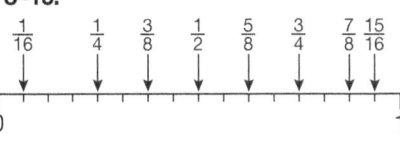

Rocket Answers will vary.

Page 19
Ordering fractions
1. $\frac{5}{12}, \frac{5}{6}$
2. $\frac{3}{5}, \frac{2}{3}$
3. $\frac{5}{6}, \frac{7}{8}$
4. $\frac{5}{12}, \frac{3}{4}, \frac{5}{6}$
5. $\frac{7}{15}, \frac{1}{2}, \frac{4}{5}$
6. $\frac{2}{21}, \frac{1}{7}, \frac{2}{3}$
7. $\frac{5}{18}, \frac{4}{9}, \frac{1}{2}$
8. $\frac{1}{2}, \frac{3}{5}, \frac{7}{10}$
9. $\frac{7}{12}, \frac{19}{24}, \frac{5}{6}$
10. $\frac{1}{3}, \frac{17}{30}, \frac{4}{5}$
11. $\frac{3}{8}, \frac{15}{24}, \frac{2}{3}$
12. $\frac{1}{5}, \frac{5}{6}, \frac{27}{30}$

Rocket Answers will vary.

13. True
14. True
15. True
16. False
17. True
18. False

Page 20
Fractions of amounts
1. $\frac{1}{2}$ of 8 = 4
   $\frac{1}{4}$ of 8 = 2
2. $\frac{1}{2}$ of 12 = 6
   $\frac{1}{3}$ of 12 = 4
   $\frac{1}{6}$ of 12 = 2
3. $\frac{1}{2}$ of 10 = 5
   $\frac{1}{5}$ of 10 = 2
4. $\frac{1}{2}$ of 18 = 9
   $\frac{1}{3}$ of 18 = 6
   $\frac{1}{6}$ of 18 = 3
5. $\frac{1}{3}$ of 12p = 4p
6. $\frac{1}{4}$ of 16p = 4p
7. $\frac{1}{2}$ of 10p = 5p
8. $\frac{1}{4}$ of 20p = 5p
9. $\frac{1}{3}$ of 12p = 4p
10. $\frac{1}{5}$ of 15p = 3p
11. $\frac{1}{2}$ of 14p = 7p
12. $\frac{1}{4}$ of 16p = 4p

Rocket 60 1p coins (or any multiple of 60).

Page 21
Fractions of amounts
1. 16 girls
2. 24 teeth
3. 13 fruit gums

Rocket Answers will vary.

Fractions, Decimals and Percentages Pupil Book 2

4. 2   5. 3   6. 1
7. 2   8. 6   9. 5

Rocket Answers will vary.

Page 22
Fractions of amounts

1. $\frac{1}{4}$ of 8 = 2
   $\frac{3}{4}$ of 8 = 6
2. $\frac{1}{3}$ of 6 = 2
   $\frac{2}{3}$ of 6 = 4
3. $\frac{1}{5}$ of 10 = 2
   $\frac{3}{5}$ of 10 = 6
4. $\frac{1}{8}$ of 16 = 2
   $\frac{5}{8}$ of 16 = 10
5. $\frac{1}{6}$ of 12 = 2
   $\frac{5}{6}$ of 12 = 10
6. $\frac{1}{10}$ of 100 = 10
   $\frac{3}{10}$ of 100 = 30
7. $\frac{1}{10}$ of £70 = £7, $\frac{3}{10}$ of £70 = £21
8. $\frac{1}{5}$ of 15 cm = 3 cm, $\frac{2}{5}$ of 15 cm = 6 cm
9. $\frac{1}{4}$ of 32 kg = 8 kg, $\frac{3}{4}$ of 32 kg = 24 kg
10. $\frac{1}{8}$ of 40 ml = 5 ml, $\frac{7}{8}$ of 40 ml = 35 ml

Rocket Answers will vary.

Page 23
Fractions of amounts

1. $\frac{1}{3}$ of 9 = 3 → $\frac{2}{3}$ of 9 = 6
2. $\frac{1}{4}$ of 12 = 3 → $\frac{3}{4}$ of 12 = 9
3. $\frac{1}{5}$ of 20 = 4 → $\frac{4}{5}$ of 20 = 16
4. $\frac{1}{6}$ of 42 = 7 → $\frac{5}{6}$ of 42 = 35
5. $\frac{1}{10}$ of 60 = 6 → $\frac{7}{10}$ of 60 = 42
6. $\frac{1}{8}$ of 64 = 8 → $\frac{3}{8}$ of 64 = 24
7. $\frac{3}{5}$ of 15 = 9
8. $\frac{3}{4}$ of 28 = 21
9. $\frac{7}{10}$ of 80 = 56
10. 2   11. 11   12. 13
13. 5   14. 3   15. 26

Rocket Answers will vary.

Page 24
Finding fractions of amounts

1. $\frac{1}{4}$ of £48 = £12, $\frac{3}{4}$ of £48 = £36
2. $\frac{1}{3}$ of £27 = £9, $\frac{2}{3}$ of £27 = £18
3. $\frac{1}{5}$ of £45 = £9, $\frac{2}{5}$ of £45 = £18
4. $\frac{1}{10}$ of £60 = £6, $\frac{3}{10}$ of £60 = £18
5. $\frac{1}{5}$ of £30 = £6, $\frac{4}{5}$ of £30 = £24
6. $\frac{1}{8}$ of £24 = £3, $\frac{3}{8}$ of £24 = £9
7. $\frac{1}{6}$ of £30 = £5, $\frac{5}{6}$ of £30 = £25
8. $\frac{1}{7}$ of £28 = £4, $\frac{4}{7}$ of £28 = £16
9. $\frac{1}{9}$ of £45 = £5, $\frac{7}{9}$ of £45 = £35

Rocket Answers will vary.

10. $\frac{1}{5}$ of £25 = £5, $\frac{3}{5}$ of £25 = £15
11. $\frac{1}{3}$ of 21 cm = 7 cm, $\frac{2}{3}$ of 21 cm = 14 cm
12. $\frac{1}{10}$ of 80 g = 8 g, $\frac{7}{10}$ of 80 g = 56 g
13. $\frac{1}{4}$ of 12 km = 3 km, $\frac{3}{4}$ of 12 km = 9 km
14. $\frac{1}{6}$ of 300 ml = 50 ml, $\frac{5}{6}$ of 300 ml = 250 ml

15. $\frac{1}{9}$ of 18 m = 2 m, $\frac{7}{9}$ of 18 m = 14 m
16. $\frac{1}{8}$ of 40 l = 5 l, $\frac{3}{8}$ of 40 l = 15 l
17. $\frac{1}{7}$ of 63 kg = 9 kg, $\frac{2}{7}$ of 63 kg = 18 kg
18. $\frac{1}{6}$ of 18 g = 3 g, $\frac{4}{6}$ of 18 g = 12 g
19. $\frac{1}{3}$ of 24 cm = 8 cm, $\frac{2}{3}$ of 24 cm = 16 cm
20. $\frac{1}{7}$ of 63 l = 9 l, $\frac{5}{7}$ of 63 l = 45 l
21. $\frac{1}{4}$ of 48 m = 12 m, $\frac{3}{4}$ of 48 m = 36 m

Page 25
Tenths

1. $\frac{3}{10}$ 2. $\frac{7}{10}$ 3. $\frac{2}{10}$
4. $\frac{6}{10}$ 5. $\frac{9}{10}$ 6. $\frac{8}{10}$
7. $\frac{2}{10}$

Each fraction expressed as a decimal:
1. 0·3   2. 0·7   3. 0·2
4. 0·6   5. 0·9   6. 0·8
7. 0·2
8. 0·6, $\frac{7}{10}$, eight tenths
9. 0·3, four tenths, $\frac{5}{10}$
10. seven tenths, $\frac{8}{10}$, 0·9
11. $\frac{3}{10}$, 0·5, 0·7
12. $\frac{5}{10}$, 0·6, $\frac{8}{10}$
13. $\frac{3}{10}$, 0·4, $\frac{1}{2}$

Rocket Answers will vary.

Page 26
Tenths

1. $1\frac{3}{10}$ 2. $3\frac{4}{10}$ 3. $2\frac{6}{10}$
4. $1\frac{9}{10}$ 5. $1\frac{7}{10}$ 6. $2\frac{1}{10}$

As decimals:
1. 1·3   2. 3·4   3. 2·6
4. 1·9   5. 1·7   6. 2·1
7. $\frac{13}{10}$ 8. $\frac{21}{10}$ 9. $\frac{36}{10}$
10. $\frac{44}{10}$ 11. $\frac{117}{10}$ 12. $\frac{35}{10}$
13. $\frac{17}{10}$ 14. $\frac{23}{10}$

Rocket $\frac{13}{10}, \frac{17}{10}, \frac{21}{10}, \frac{23}{10}, \frac{35}{10}, \frac{36}{10}, \frac{44}{10}, \frac{117}{10}$
Answers will vary.

Page 27
Tenths

1. a: 1·8   b: 3·1
   c: 1·3   d: 0·2
   e: 2·8   f: 3·5
   g: 0·6   h: 2·4
2. 2·3 tubs   3. 4·7 tubs
4. 1·6 tubs   5. 3·8 tubs
6. 5·4 tubs   7. 7·9 tubs

For a complete number of tubs:
2. 7 more tokens
3. 3 more tokens
4. 4 more tokens
5. 2 more tokens
6. 6 more tokens
7. 1 more token

Rocket Six numbers can be made between 3·3 and 7·3: 3·5, 3·7, 5·2, 5·3, 5·7, 7·2.
Five numbers can be made outside this range: 2·3, 2·5, 2·7, 3·2, 7·5.
The whole set in order: 2·3, 2·5, 2·7, 3·2, 3·5, 3·7, 5·2, 5·3, 5·7, 7·2, 7·3, 7·5.

Page 28
Hundredths

1. £6·59
2. £4·72
3. £7·25
4. £8·98
5. £3·64
6. £1·13
7. £1·13, £3·64, £4·72, £6·59, £7·25, £8·98
8. b   9. a   10. f
11. c   12. h   13. e
14. d   15. j   16. g
17. i

Rocket Seven numbers: 1·51, 1·61, 1·71, 1·81, 1·91, 2·01, 2·11
Six numbers: 1·52, 1·62, 1·72, 1·82, 1·92, 2·02

Page 29
Tenths and hundredths

1. $\frac{35}{100}$ = 0·35
2. $\frac{76}{100}$ = 0·76
3. $\frac{18}{100}$ = 0·18
4. $\frac{24}{100}$ = 0·24
5. $\frac{92}{100}$ = 0·92
6. $\frac{47}{100}$ = 0·47

Rocket Answers will vary.

7. 37 hundredths = $\frac{3}{10} + \frac{7}{100}$
8. $\frac{46}{100}$ = 4 tenths + 6 hundredths
9. $2\frac{64}{100} = 2 + \frac{6}{10} + \frac{4}{100}$
10. 74 hundredths = $\frac{7}{10} + \frac{4}{100}$
11. $4\frac{32}{100} = 4 + \frac{3}{10} + \frac{2}{100}$

Page 30
Tenths and hundredths

1. 80 hundredths = 8 tenths
2. 17 tenths = 170 hundredths
3. 320 hundredths = 32 tenths
4. 100 tenths = 1000 hundredths
5. 4 units
6. 1 tenth
7. 8 tenths
8. 4 hundredths
9. 7 units
10. 4 tenths
11. 0 hundredths
12. 3 tens
13. 3 tenths
14. 8 hundredths
15. 7 units
16. 6 hundredths
17. 4 tenths

18. 9 tens
19. 2 units
20. 6 hundredths
21. True
22. True
23. False
24. False
25. True
26. True
27. 5 tenths
28. 6 tenths + 9 hundredths
29. 7 units + 5 tenths + 6 hundredths

Rocket 3·07 = 3 units + 0 tenths + 7 hundredths
3·7 = 3 units + 7 tenths

Page 31
Ordering decimals

1. Running: Vijay, Swimming: Sufia, Cycling: Chang
2. Running: Sufia, Swimming: Emma, Cycling: Sufia
3. Running: Emma, Swimming: Vijay, Cycling: Josh
4. Running: Josh, Swimming: Chang, Cycling: Scott
5. Running: Chang, Swimming: Kim, Cycling: Scott
6. Running: Chang, Swimming: Vijay, Cycling: Kim
7. Running: 0·42 seconds, Swimming: 0·77 seconds, Cycling: 1·44 seconds
8. Sufia
9–14. Answers will vary.

Rocket 6·0, 6·04, 6·07, 6·4, 6·47, 6·7, 6·74, 7·0, 7·04, 7·06, 7·4, 7·46, 7·6, 7·64

Page 32
Rounding

1. a: 4·2 → 4
   b: 4·9 → 5
   c: 4·4 → 4
   d: 4·6 → 5
2. e: 10·5 → 11
   f: 10·7 → 11
   g: 10·1 → 10
   h: 10·4 → 10
3. i: 0·8 → 1
   j: 0·3 → 0
   k: 0·5 → 1
4. 6·3 kg → 6 kg
5. 8·4 kg → 8 kg
6. 4·9 kg → 5 kg
7. 7·2 kg → 7 kg
8. 2·3 kg → 2 kg
9. 6·6 kg → 7 kg
10. 5·5 kg → 6 kg
11. 11·7 kg → 12 kg
12. 8·8 kg → 9 kg

Rocket Cats 4 and 10, 6 and 7, 6 and 9, or 9 and 10

Page 33
Rounding

1. 6·2 cm → 6 cm
   4·5 cm → 5 cm
   4·9 cm → 5 cm
   10·7 cm → 11 cm
   3·2 cm → 3 cm
   4·6 cm → 5 cm
   6·5 cm → 7 cm

Rocket Answers will vary.

2. a: 2·62 → 3
   b: 2·4 → 2
   c: 2·86 → 3
   d: 2·17 → 2
   e: 2·49 → 2
   f: 6·76 → 7
   g: 6·09 → 6
   h: 6·92 → 7
   i: 6·35 → 6
   j: 6·53 → 7

Page 34
Rounding

1. £4·76 → £5
2. £5·23 → £5
3. £1·47 → £1
4. £3·56 → £4
5. £2·39 → £2
6. £4·85 → £5
7. £7·09 → £7
8. £5·97 → £6
9. £60·10 → £60
10. £4·50 → £5
11. £0·82 → £1
12. £1·04 → £1
13. £2·22 → £2
14. £0·34 → £0

Rocket Answers will vary.

Page 35
Rounding

1. a: 4·42 → 4
      4·42 → 4·4
   b: 4·72 → 5
      4·72 → 4·7
   c: 4·08 → 4
      4·08 → 4·1
   d: 4·57 → 5
      4·57 → 4·6
   e: 4·18 → 4
      4·18 → 4·2
   f: 4·84 → 5
      4·84 → 4·8
2. g: 26·29 → 26
      26·29 → 26·3
   h: 26·94 → 27
      26·94 → 26·9
   i: 26·45 → 26
      26·45 → 26·5
   j: 26·78 → 27
      26·78 → 26·8
   k: 26·14 → 26
      26·14 → 26·1
   l: 26·62 → 27
      26·62 → 26·6
3. 34·62 m → 35 m
   34·62 m → 34·6 m
4. 18·49 m → 18 m
   18·49 m → 18·5 m
5. 13·27 m → 13 m
   13·27 m → 13·3 m
6. 25·34 m → 25 m
   25·34 m → 25·3 m
7. 11·08 m → 11 m
   11·08 m → 11·1 m
8. 19·46 m → 19 m
   19·46 m → 19·5 m

Rocket Smallest difference = 5·01 m; Largest difference = 6·99 m

Page 36
Rounding

1. £8·38 → a: £8   b: £8·40
2. £14·52 → a: £15   b: £14·50
3. £26·35 → a: £26   b: £26·40
4. £9·18 → a: £9   b: £9·20
5. £32·41 → a £32   b: £32·40
6. £18·76 → a: £19   b: £18·80
7. £48·48 → a: £48   b: £48·50
8. £32·91 → a: £33   b: £32·90
9. £16·85 → a: £17   b: £16·90
10. £25·36 → a: £25   b: £25·40
11. £17·18 → a: £17   b: £17·20
12. £42·67 → a: £43   b: £42·70
13. £58·76 → a: £59   b: £58·80
14. £47·43 → a: £47   b: £47·40
15. £25·23 → a: £25   b: £25·20
16. £26·36 → a: £26   b: £26·40
17. £73·84 → a: £74   b: £73·80
18. £59·85 → a: £60   b: £59·90
19. £27·94 → a: £28   b: £27·90
20. £59·26 → a: £59   b: £59·30
21. £41·59 → a: £42   b: £41·60

Rocket The answers are not necessarily the same. For example, with question 14, the total rounds to £47 (to the nearest pound) but if the sums are rounded first (£15 and £33) they total £48.

Page 37
Rounding

1. 12·37 s → 12 s
2. 11·59 s → 12 s
3. 12·88 s → 13 s
4. 13·36 s → 13 s
5. 15·64 s → 16 s
6. 14·49 s → 14 s
7. 28 s
8. 28 s
9. 28 s
10. Ben and Den
11. Tim and Kim
12. Kat and Pat

Rocket Answers will vary. Ruth could have an amount over £4 which, when added to Ian's amount over £6, gives a total over £10·50. Similarly, they could both have amounts under £4 and £6, that when added together give a total under £9·50.

Page 38
Multiplying by 10, 100 and 1000

1. 2·3 = 2 units + 3 tenths
   2·3 × 10 = (2 units × 10) + (3 tenths × 10)
   = 20 + 3
   = 23
2. 4·8 = 4 units + 8 tenths
   4·8 × 10 = (4 units × 10) + (8 tenths × 10)
   = 40 + 8
   = 48
3. 3·6 = 3 units + 6 tenths
   3·6 × 10 = (3 units × 10) + (6 tenths × 10)
   = 30 + 6
   = 36
4. 3·4 = 3 units + 4 tenths
   3·4 × 10 = (3 units × 10) + (4 tenths × 10)
   = 30 + 4
   = 34
5. 5·7 = 5 units + 7 tenths
   5·7 × 10 = (5 units × 10) + (7 tenths × 10)
   = 50 + 7
   = 57
6. 8·6 = 8 units + 6 tenths
   8·6 × 10 = (8 units × 10) + (6 tenths × 10)
   = 80 + 6
   = 86
7. 14·2 = 1 ten + 4 units + 2 tenths
   14·2 × 10 = (1 ten × 10) + (4 units × 10) + (2 tenths × 10)
   = 100 + 40 + 2
   = 142
8. 12·5 = 1 ten + 2 units + 5 tenths
   12·5 × 10 = (1 ten × 10) + (2 units × 10) + (5 tenths × 10)
   = 100 + 20 + 5
   = 125
9. 17·6 = 1 ten + 7 units + 6 tenths
   17·6 × 10 = (1 ten × 10) + (7 units × 10) + (6 tenths × 10)
   = 100 + 70 + 6
   = 176
10. 20·7 = 2 tens + 7 tenths
    20·7 × 10 = (2 tens × 10) + (7 tenths × 10)
    = 200 + 7
    = 207
11. 44·8 = 4 tens + 4 units + 8 tenths
    44·8 × 10 = (4 tens × 10) + (4 units × 10) + (8 tenths × 10)
    = 400 + 40 + 8
    = 448

Rocket Answers will vary.

12. 3·7 = 3 units and 7 tenths
    3·7 × 100 = (3 units × 100) + (7 tenths × 100)
    = 300 + 70
    = 370
13. 8·6 = 8 units and 6 tenths
    8·6 × 100 = (8 units × 100) + (6 tenths × 100)
    = 800 + 60
    = 860
14. 4·57 = 4 units and 5 tenths and 7 hundredths
    4·57 × 100 = (4 units × 100) + (5 tenths × 100) + (7 hundredths × 100)
    = 400 + 50 + 7
    = 457
15. 10·35 = 1 ten and 3 tenths and 5 hundredths
    10·35 × 100 = (1 ten × 100) + (3 tenths × 100) + (5 hundredths × 100)
    = 1000 + 30 + 5
    = 1035
16. 7·06 × 100 = 706
17. 38·07 × 100 = 3807
18. 40·06 × 100 = 4006
19. 105·07 × 100 = 10 507

Rocket Answers will vary.

Page 39
Multiplying by 10, 100 and 1000

1. £5·50 × 10 = £55
2. £3·40 × 10 = £34
3. £10·50 × 10 = £105
4. £6·65 × 10 = £66·50
5. £4·44 × 10 = £44·40
6. £7·75 × 10 = £77·50
7. £3·29 × 10 = £32·90
8. £6·25 × 10 = £62·50
9. £5·46 × 10 = £54·60
10. £10·33 × 10 = £103·30
11. £8·66 × 10 = £86·60

Wages for doing each job 100 times:

1. £5·50 × 100 = £550
2. £3·40 × 100 = £340
3. £10·50 × 100 = £1050
4. £6·65 × 100 = £665
5. £4·44 × 100 = £444
6. £7·75 × 100 = £775
7. £3·29 × 100 = £329
8. £6·25 × 100 = £625
9. £5·46 × 100 = £546
10. £10·33 × 100 = £1033
11. £8·66 × 100 = £866
12. True
13. False
14. False
15. True
16. False

Rocket Multiplying £5·50 by 10 five times = £550 000, less than £1 000 000.

Page 40
Multiplying by 10, 100 and 1000

1. 3·64 m = (3·64 × 100) cm = 364 cm
2. 4·8 m × 100 = (4·8 × 100) cm = 480 cm
3. 2·08 m × 100 = (2·08 × 100) cm = 208 cm
4. 14·07 m × 100 = (14·07 × 100) cm = 1407 cm
5. 0·86 m × 100 = (0·86 × 100) cm = 86 cm
6. 0·24 m × 100 = (0·24 × 100) cm = 24 cm
7. 13·06 × 1000 = 13 060
8. 20·08 × 100 = 2008
9. 203·4 × 100 = 20 340
10. 345·04 × 1000 = 345 040
11. 10 × 195·3 = 1953
12. 38·06 × 1000 = 38 060

Rocket Nine amounts between £1 and £2 (10p, 20p, 30p, ...); 89 amounts between £1 and £10 (£1·10, £1·20, £1·30, ...).

Page 41
Dividing by 10, 100 and 1000

1. 507p = £(507 ÷ 100) = £5·07
2. 643p = £(643 ÷ 100) = £6·43
3. 777p = £(777 ÷ 100) = £7·77
4. 1004p = £(1004 ÷ 100) = £10·04
5. 990p = £(990 ÷ 100) = £9·90
6. 7040p = £(7040 ÷ 100) = £70·40
7. 101p = £(101 ÷ 100) = £1·01
8. 2301p = £(2301 ÷ 100) = £23·01
9. 648p = £(648 ÷ 100) = £6·48
10. 3709p = £(3709 ÷ 100) = £37·09
11. 876p = £(876 ÷ 100) = £8·76
12. 2500p = £(2500 ÷ 100) = £25·00

Rocket Answers will vary.

13. 1400 m = (1400 ÷ 1000) km = 1·4 km
14. 4780 m = (4780 ÷ 1000) km = 4·78 km
15. 3660 ml = (3660 ÷ 1000) l = 3·66 l
16. 700 ml = (700 ÷ 1000) l = 0·7 l
17. 4880 g = (4880 ÷ 1000) kg = 4·88 kg
18. 5700 m = (5700 ÷ 1000) km = 5·7 km
19. 6990 ml = (6990 ÷ 1000) ml = 6·99 l
20. 4820 kg = (4820 ÷ 1000) kg = 4·82 kg
21. 3650 m = (3650 ÷ 1000) m = 3·65 km

Page 42
Dividing by 10, 100 and 1000

1. 4260 ÷ 100 = 42·6
   42 100 g weights
   6 10 g weights

2. $33\,790 \div 100 = 337.9$
   337 100 g weights
   9 10 g weights
3. $5470 \div 100 = 54.7$
   54 100 g weights
   7 10 g weights
4. $2180 \div 100 = 21.8$
   21 100 g weights
   8 10 g weights
5. $6190 \div 100 = 61.9$
   61 100 g weights
   9 10 g weights
6. $48\,210 \div 100 = 482.1$
   482 100 g weights
   1 10 g weight
7. $3940 \div 100 = 39.4$
   39 100 g weights
   4 10 g weights
8. $12\,590 \div 100 = 125.9$
   125 100 g weights
   9 10 g weights
9. $3010 \div 1000 = 3.01$
10. $41.36 \div 1000 = 0.04136$
11. $38.9 \div 10 = 3.89$
12. $36 \div 100 = 0.36$
13. $90.9 \div 1000 = 0.0909$
14. $584.2 \div 10 = 58.42$
15. $0.2 \div 10 = 0.02$
16. $63.4 \div 10 = 6.34$
17. £10·40; £20·80
18. 1·345 m
19. 2046 notes; 204·6 bundles

Page 43
Percentages

1. 60%   2. 30%   3. 15%
4. 75%   5. 40%   6. 22%
7. 83%   8. 57%

Not coloured:
1. 40%   2. 70%   3. 85%
4. 25%   5. 60%   6. 78%
7. 17%   8. 43%

Rocket Answers will vary.

9. 80%   10. 10%   11. 45%
12. 95%   13. 1%   14. 50%
15. 25%   16. 75%   17. 20%
18. 70%

19–22. The second fraction may vary.
19. $\frac{30}{100} = \frac{3}{10}$ 20. $\frac{25}{100} = \frac{1}{4}$
21. $\frac{90}{100} = \frac{9}{10}$ 22. $\frac{20}{100} = \frac{2}{10} = \frac{1}{5}$

Page 44
Percentages

1. $\frac{1}{2}$, 0·5, 50%   2. $\frac{1}{4}$, 0·25, 25%
3. $\frac{1}{10}$, 0·1, 10%   4. $\frac{3}{4}$, 0·75, 75%
5. $\frac{3}{5}$, 0·6, 60%   6. $\frac{7}{10}$, 0·7, 70%
7. $\frac{4}{5}$, 0·8, 80%   8. $\frac{9}{10}$, 0·9, 90%

Not coloured;
1. 50%   2. 75%   3. 90%
4. 25%   5. 40%   6. 30%
7. 20%   8. 10%

Rocket 12 squares are not coloured

15% of the shape is not coloured.
Answers will vary.

Page 45
Percentages of amounts

1. £20   2. £40   3. £54
4. £60   5. £95   6. £12
7. £20   8. £34

Rocket 2·5%, 5%, 7·5%, 10%, 12·5%,
15%, 17·5%, 20%...97·5%

9. 1st prize £25
   2nd prize £12·50
   3rd prize £5
10. 1st prize £60
    2nd prize £30
    3rd prize £12
11. 1st prize £100
    2nd prize £50
    3rd prize £20
12. 1st prize £40
    2nd prize £20
    3rd prize £8
13. 1st prize £500
    2nd prize £250
    3rd prize £100

9–13. 15% is left each time.
9. £7·50
10. £18
11. £30
12. £12
13. £150

Page 46
Percentages of amounts

1. 10% of £14 = £1·40
2. 10% of £11 = £1·10
3. 10% of £12 = £1·20
4. 10% of £5 = 50p
5. 10% of £13 = £1·30
6. 10% of £8 = 80p
7. 10% of £9 = 90p
8. 10% of £15 = £1·50

20% of each price:
1. 20% of £14 = £2·80
2. 20% of £11 = £2·20
3. 20% of £12 = £2·40
4. 20% of £5 = £1·00
5. 20% of £13 = £2·60
6. 20% of £8 = £1·60
7. 20% of £9 = £1·80
8. 20% of £15 = £3·00
9. 14 m = 1400 cm
   10% of 1400 cm = 140 cm
10. 7 m = 700 cm
    10% of 700 cm = 70 cm
11. 6 m = 600 cm
    10% of 600 cm = 60 cm
12. 4 m = 400 cm
    10% of 400 cm = 40 cm
13. 10% of 750 cm = 75 cm
14. 8 m = 800 cm
    10% of 800 cm = 80 cm
15. 10% of 3400 cm = 340 cm

16. 22 m = 2200 cm
    10% of 2200 cm = 220 cm
17. 18 m = 1800 cm
    10% of 1800 cm = 180 cm
18. 10% of 230 cm = 23 cm
19. 54 m = 5400 cm
    10% of 5400 cm = 540 cm
20. 10% of 1200 cm = 120 cm

Rocket Answers will vary.

Page 47
Percentages of amounts

1. $\frac{1}{2}$ = 50%
   $\frac{1}{4}$ = 25%
   $\frac{1}{5}$ = 20%
   $\frac{3}{4}$ = 75%
   $\frac{1}{100}$ = 1%
   $\frac{1}{10}$ = 10%
   $\frac{1}{8}$ = 12·5%
2. Greater reduction: 20% of £20
3. Greater reduction: 50% of £10
4. Greater reduction: 60% of £22
5. Greater reduction: 10% of £30

Rocket It is impossible to make more
than 100% effort, as 100% is
the whole.

Page 48
Percentages of amounts

1. 50% = $\frac{1}{2}$ 2. 25% = $\frac{1}{4}$
3. 10% = $\frac{1}{10}$ 4. 20% = $\frac{1}{5}$
5. 70% = $\frac{7}{10}$ 6. 75% = $\frac{3}{4}$
7. 100% = 1   8. 5% = $\frac{1}{20}$
9. $200 \div 10 = 20$
   10% of 200 = 20
10. $360 \div 10 = 36$
    10% of 360 = 36
11. $580 \div 10 = 58$
    10% of 580 = 58
12. $240 \div 10 = 24$
    10% of 240 = 24
13. $1250 \div 10 = 125$
    10% of 1250 = 125
14. $2840 \div 10 = 284$
    10% of 2840 = 284
15. $3690 \div 10 = 369$
    10% of 3690 = 369
16. $3570 \div 10 = 357$
    10% of 3570 = 357

30% of the amounts
9. 30% of 200 = 3 × 20 = 60
10. 30% of 360 = 3 × 36 = 108
11. 30% of 580 = 3 × 58 = 174
12. 30% of 240 = 3 × 24 = 72
13. 30% of 1250 = 3 × 125 = 375
14. 30% of 2840 = 3 × 284 = 852
15. 30% of 3690 = 3 × 369 = 1107
16. 30% of 3570 = 3 × 357 = 1071
17. 25% of 200 = 50
18. 25% of 440 = 110
19. 25% of 560 = 140

20. 25% of 480 = 120
21. 25% of 1640 = 410
22. 25% of 2960 = 740
23. 25% of 3960 = 990
24. 25% of 3580 = 895

75% of the amounts:
17. 75% of 200 = 150
18. 75% of 440 = 330
19. 75% of 560 = 420
20. 75% of 480 = 360
21. 75% of 1640 = 1230
22. 75% of 2960 = 2220
23. 75% of 3960 = 2970
24. 75% of 3580 = 2685

Rocket Answers will vary.

Page 49
Remainders

1. 14 teams 1 left over
2. 5 teams 2 left over
3. 10 teams 2 left over
4. 7 teams 4 left over
5. 6 teams 1 left over
6. 7 teams 7 left over
7. 9 teams 4 left over
8. 7 teams 5 left over
9. 8 teams 1 left over

Rocket To make teams without any remainders, choose a number of players that is a multiple of the team size. For example, teams of 3 can be made from 3, 6, 9, … players.

10–21. Answers will vary.

Page 50
Dividing

1. $5\frac{1}{2}$
2. $8\frac{1}{4}$
3. $8\frac{2}{5}$
4. $7\frac{2}{3}$
5. $3\frac{1}{6}$
6. $4\frac{3}{7}$
7. $4\frac{7}{10}$
8. $3\frac{2}{9}$
9. $6\frac{2}{8}$ (or $6\frac{1}{4}$)
10. $6\frac{3}{4}$
11. $7\frac{3}{6}$ (or $7\frac{1}{2}$)
12. $9\frac{4}{9}$

Rocket Answers will vary.

13. $43 \div 2 = 21\frac{1}{2}$
14. $43 \div 3 = 14\frac{1}{3}$
15. $43 \div 4 = 10\frac{3}{4}$
16. $43 \div 5 = 8\frac{3}{5}$
17. $43 \div 6 = 7\frac{1}{6}$
18. $43 \div 7 = 6\frac{1}{7}$
19. $43 \div 8 = 5\frac{3}{8}$
20. $43 \div 9 = 4\frac{7}{9}$
21. $43 \div 10 = 4\frac{3}{10}$

For 67 macaroons:
13. $67 \div 2 = 33\frac{1}{2}$
14. $67 \div 3 = 22\frac{1}{3}$
15. $67 \div 4 = 16\frac{3}{4}$
16. $67 \div 5 = 13\frac{2}{5}$
17. $67 \div 6 = 11\frac{1}{6}$
18. $67 \div 7 = 9\frac{4}{7}$
19. $67 \div 8 = 8\frac{3}{8}$
20. $67 \div 9 = 7\frac{4}{9}$
21. $67 \div 10 = 6\frac{7}{10}$

Page 51
Dividing

1. 3·1
2. 7·6
3. 21·5
4. 40·5
5. 4·25
6. 8·25
7. 2·4
8. 5·6
9. 1·4
10. 8·5
11. 6·4
12. 9·4
13. 7
14. 12 with 1 pigeon left over.
15. 7
16. 7
17.

	27	33	81	55	103
÷ 10	2·7	3·3	8·1	5·5	10·3
÷ 2	13·5	16·5	40·5	27·5	51·5
÷ 4	6·75	8·25	20·25	13·75	25·75
÷ 5	5·4	6·6	16·2	11	20·6

Page 52
Adding

1. 5·8 + 4·2 = 10
2. 6·2 + 3·8 = 10
3. 4·8 + 5·2 = 10
4. 5·3 + 4·7 = 10
5. 6·1 + 3·9 = 10
6. 0·7 + 9·3 = 10
7. 6·6 + 3·4 = 10
8. 4·8 + 5·2 = 10
9. 2·7 + 7·3 = 10
10. 5·2 m
11. 3·6 m
12. 4·3 m
13. 5·7 m
14. 6·8 m
15. 1·9 m
16. 7·2 m
17. 2·4 m

Rocket Six £1 coins and two £2 coins; or nine £1 coins and two 50p coins.

Page 53
Adding

1. 1·3 + 0·7 = 2 m
2. 2·8 + 0·2 = 3 m
3. 4·5 + 0·5 = 5 m
4. 3·6 + 0·4 = 4 m
5. 5·6 + 0·4 = 6 m
6. 2·4 + 0·6 = 3 m
7. 6·3 + 0·7 = 7 m
8. 4·9 + 0·1 = 5 m
9. 5·2 + 0·8 = 6 m
10. 3·2 + 0·8 = 4 m
11. 1·8 + 0·2 = 2 m
12. 7·6 + 0·4 = 8 m

Rocket Answers will vary.
13. 5·4 + 4·6 = 10 m
    7·3 + 2·7 = 10 m
    6·8 + 3·2 = 10 m
    1·8 + 8·2 = 10 m
    5·2 + 4·8 = 10 m
14. 4·6 + 0·7 = 5·3
15. 3·8 + 0·5 = 4·3
16. 2·7 + 0·6 = 3·3
17. 5·5 + 0·8 = 6·3
18. 6·3 + 0·6 = 6·9
19. 3·5 + 0·8 = 4·3

Page 54
Adding

1. 3·6 + 0·4 = 4 kg
2. 2·8 + 0·2 = 3 kg
3. 5·4 + 0·6 = 6 kg
4. 6·2 + 0·8 = 7 kg
5. 4·3 + 0·7 = 5 kg
6. 6·7 + 0·3 = 7 kg
7. 3·1 + 0·9 = 4 kg
8. 5·9 + 0·1 = 6 kg
9. 1·2 + 1·7 = 2·9 kg
10. 2·3 + 4·6 = 6·9 kg
11. 1·6 + 2·8 = 4·4 kg
12. 2·8 + 3·7 = 6·5 kg
13. 1·8 + 1·5 = 3·3 kg
14. 2·7 + 1·9 = 4·6 kg
15. 16·2 km
16. 6·1 m
17. 32·4 kg
18. 2·4 + 3·8 = 6·2
19. 3·7 + 2·4 = 6·1
20. 6·4 + 2·8 = 9·2
21. 5·3 + 2·6 = 7·9
22. 3·6 + 5·5 = 9·1
23. 2·5 + 2·7 = 5·2
24. 4·8 + 3·6 = 8·4
25. 2·8 + 3·9 = 6·7
26. 7·6 + 1·5 = 9·1

Page 55
Adding

1. ⑤
   ```
     U · t
     1 · 6
   + 2 · 7
   -------
     4 · 3
       1
   ```
2. 9·5
3. 17·2
4. 14·2
5. 14·1
6. 11·2
7. 12·1
8.
   ```
        4 · 6
   +    5 · 8
   ----------
      1 0 · 4  cm
          1
   ```
9. 13·4 cm
10. 10·5 cm

11. 13·7 cm
12. Most shelf space: Footy Facts and Fairy Tales (14·6 cm).
    Least shelf space: Dictionary and Monster Mayhem (8·4 cm).
Rocket Answers will vary.

Page 56
Subtracting

1. ① cm
   ```
     ⁴
     5·¹2
   − 3· 6
   ─────
     1· 6 cm
   ```
2. 1·6 cm
3. 1·6 cm
4. 3·7 cm
5. 0·4 cm
6. 2·9 cm
7. 2·8 cm
8. 1·9 cm
9. 1·4
10. 1·4
11. 0·6
12. 2·8
13. 3·4
14. 0·2

Page 57
Subtracting

1. ②
   ```
     ³
     4·¹3
   − 2· 5
   ─────
     1· 8
   ```
2. 2·4
3. 4·6
4. 3·9
5. 5·2
6. 1·6
7. 5·1
8. 3·6
9. 2·9
10. 3·3
Rocket 5·3 − 2·5 = 2·8
11. 0·7 m
12. 2·0 m
13. 2·0 m
14. 1·5 m
15. 1·3 m
16. 2·8 m
17. 1·2 m
18. 0·8 m

Page 58
Subtracting

1. ㊆
   ```
       ⁷¹⁵
     8 6·¹7
   −    9·8
   ──────
     7 6· 9 litres
   ```
2. 18 litres
3. 50·4 litres
4. 58·7 litres
5. 66·7 litres
6. 36·5 litres
7. 55·6 litres
8. 46·8 litres
Rocket In the tenths column the smaller digit has been subtracted from the larger digit, rather than 'borrowing' from the units column. Correct answers: 0·9; 1·6.
9. 23·7 miles
10. 64·5 m
11. 4 kg

Page 59
Subtracting

1. 2·2
2. 4·8
3. 1·5
4. 4·4
5. 3·1
6. 4·8
7. 3·5
8. 2·4
9. 1·2
10. 0·8
11. 2·9
12. 3·7
13. 6·1
14. 0·4
15. 3·9
16. 0·5 km
17. 0·2 km
18. 0·9 km
19. 1·1 km
20. 2·8 km
21. 0·4 km
Rocket Anna ran 5·2 km and Tom ran 4·8 km.

Page 60
Adding

1. ⑦
   ```
     3·3 2
   + 4·1 8
   ──────
     7·5 0
        ¹
   ```
2. 10·56
3. 7·21
4. 8·27
5. 5·92
6. 8·16
7. 7·72
8. 9·82
9. 7·24
10. 6·65
11. 6·49
12. 6·21 l
13. 7·51 l
14. 4·84 l
15. 8·88 l
16. 5·59 l
17. 8·34 l
Rocket Ten ways: 3·96 + 1·04; 3·86 + 1·14; 3·76 + 1·24; 3·66 + 1·34; 3·56 + 1·44; 3·46 + 1·54; 3·36 + 1·64; 3·26 + 1·74; 3·16 + 1·84; 3·06 + 1·94

Page 61
Adding

1. ⑫
   ```
     5·0 6
     3·7
   + 2·8 5
   ──────
   1 1·6 1
     ¹ ¹
   ```
2. 10·57
3. 7·72
4. 9·37
5. 9·56
6. 12·88
7. 19·17
8. 9·30 or 9·3
9. 15·81 kg
10. 16·43 kg
11. 19·01 kg
12. 13·91 kg
13. 17·74 kg
14. 14·35 kg
Rocket
9. 4·19 kg
10. 3·57 kg
11. 0·99 kg
12. 6·09 kg
13. 2·26 kg
14. 5·65 kg

Page 62
Adding

1. £50·89
2. £78·47
3. £54·47
4. £74·89
5. £86·69
6. £88·31
7. £54·48
8. £57·97
9. 7·83 kg
10. Pays £10·99; gets £9·01 change
11. £5·38
Rocket Answers will vary.

Page 63
Adding

1. ⑧
   ```
     5·0 7
     0·6 5
   + 1·8
   ──────
     7·5 2
     ¹ ¹
   ```
2. ⑨
   ```
     3·7 5
     4·8 6
   + 0·0 7
   ──────
     8·6 8
     ¹ ¹
   ```
3. ⑫
   ```
     4·0 8
     3·9
   + 4·2 4
   ──────
   1 2·2 2
     ¹ ¹
   ```
4. ⑥
   ```
     1·4
     3·6 5
   + 0·7 9
   ──────
     5·8 4
     ¹ ¹
   ```
5. ⑬
   ```
     6·3
     4·0 9
   + 3·2 7
   ──────
   1 3·6 6
        ¹
   ```
6. ⑫
   ```
     6·0 9
     1·8
   + 4·0 6
   ──────
   1 1·9 5
        ¹
   ```
7. ⑮
   ```
     5·1
     3·7
   + 6·0 8
   ──────
   1 4·8 8
   ```
8. ⑬
   ```
     3·2 8
     7·0 7
   + 2·8
   ──────
   1 3·1 5
     ¹ ¹
   ```

Rocket Answers will vary.
9. False 10. False 11. False

Page 64
Adding

1. Answers will vary.
2.
    ```
        £ 9·87
        £ 7·64
      + £ 7·38
      ───────
       £24·89
          1 1
    ```
3.
    ```
        £ 4·59
        £ 5·57
      + £ 5·68
      ───────
       £15·84
          1 2
    ```

Rocket The CDs costing £9·87 and £4·59

4. 16·47 m
5. £31·60
6. 16·9 km
7. 14·68 + 25·59 = 40·27
8. 23·95 + 36·87 = 60·82
9. 48·84 + 36·97 = 85·81
10. 55·97 + 43·85 = 99·82
11. 12·59 + 8 + 7·3 = 27·89
12. 14·53 + 9·17 = 23·7
13. 3·82 + 10·37 + 1·66 = 15·85
14. 4·25 + 12·68 + 3·27 = 20·2

Page 65
Adding

1.
    ```
       36·47
    +   5·69
    ────────
       42·16
        1 1
    ```
2.
    ```
      117·85
    +  17·76
    ────────
      135·61
       1 1 1
    ```
3.
    ```
       16·58
    +  43·07
    ────────
       59·65
           1
    ```
4.
    ```
       27·63
    +   4·42
    ────────
       32·05
        1 1
    ```
5.
    ```
       18·92
    +  16·38
    ────────
       35·30
        1 1 1
    ```
6.
    ```
       42·89
    +  19·24
    ────────
       62·13
        1 1
    ```
7.
    ```
       47·36
    +  21·29
    ────────
       68·65
           1
    ```
8.
    ```
       61·27
    +  12·86
    ────────
       74·13
        1 1
    ```
9.
    ```
       37·85
    +  22·31
    ────────
       60·16
        1 1
    ```
10.
    ```
       12·38
    +   9·42
    ────────
       21·80
        1 1
    ```
11.
    ```
       18·27
    +  24·96
    ────────
       43·23
        1 1 1
    ```
12.
    ```
       21·65
    +  18·78
    ────────
       40·43
        1 1 1
    ```
13.
    ```
       32·79
    +   4·73
    ────────
       37·52
        1 1
    ```
14.
    ```
       27·34
    +  16·83
    ────────
       44·17
        1 1
    ```
15.
    ```
       54·38
    +  27·46
    ────────
       81·84
        1 1
    ```
16.
    ```
       67·54
    +   8·95
    ────────
       76·49
        1 1
    ```

Rocket Answers may vary. It is possible to reach 10 exactly. One solution is:
```
    3·79
  + 6·21
  ──────
   10·00
     1 1
```

Page 66
Subtracting

1. (70)
   ```
       7 16 1
       8̷ 7̷·5 6̷
     - 1 8·7 4
     ─────────
       6 8·8 2 kg
   ```
2. 68·5 kg
3. 33·8 kg
4. 64·6 kg
5. 35·65 kg
6. 35·7 kg
7. 58·92 kg
8. 57·7 kg
9. 36·73 kg
10. Answers will vary.

Rocket Children will always get an answer with repeating digits.

Page 67
Subtracting

Children's methods may vary.

1. £3·23
   £1·86 + £0·14 = £2·00
   £2·00 + £1·23 = £3·23
   £1·37
2. £1·57
3. £0·58
4. £1·33
5. £1·26
6. £1·68
7. £1·39
8. £1·53
9. £1·47

Rocket Answers will vary. For example: original price is £5·00, sale price is £3·75.

10. £2·28
11. £3·54
12. £4·37
13. £3·06
14. £1·51
15. £0·82
16. £3·29
17. £2·85

Page 68
Subtracting

Children's methods may vary.

1. £4·60
   £2·80 + £0·20 = £3·00
   £3·00 + £1·60 = £4·60
   £1·80
2. £0·90
3. £1·40
4. £1·80
5. £0·90
6. £0·50
7. £1·80
8. £3·20
9. £2·10
10. £1·11
11. £1·17
12. £2·09
13. £2·17
14. £1·11
15. £2·14
16. £2·11

Rocket £9·99 can be subtracted 10 times from £100. 10p is left over.

Page 69
Subtracting

Children's methods may vary.

1. (£6)
   ```
      £ 1 1·3 8
    - £    4·8 6
    ───────────
      £    6·5 2
   ```

2. £7·82
3. £5·27
4. £3·46
5. £4·82
6. £8·33
7. £0·51
8. £3·06
9. £1·36

Rocket Answers may vary. Children should be able to get within 0·02 of 5, for example: 8·61 − 3·59 = 5·02.

10. £4·75
11. £8·87
12. £16·34
13. £10·53
14. £11·86
15. £5·79

Page 70
Subtracting

Here are the corrections to Lucy's homework:

1. $1\;^11\;^14$
    $2\;\bcancel{2}\;\bcancel{5}\;^13$
    $-8\;\;8\;\;4$
    $1\;3\;6\;9$

2. $^12\;^13$
    $\bcancel{3}\;\bcancel{4}\;^12$
    $-\;\;7\;\;8\;\;9$
    $\;\;5\;5\;3$

3. Correct

4. $5\;^12\;^1$
    $\bcancel{6}\;\bcancel{3}\;\bcancel{2}\;^14$
    $-\;\;7\;9\;5$
    $\;\;5\;5\;2\;9$

5. Correct

6. $2\;^15\;^13$
    $\bcancel{3}\;\bcancel{6}\;\bcancel{4}\;^12$
    $-\;\;7\;7\;8$
    $\;\;2\;8\;6\;4$

7. 12·34
    − 7·78
    ──────
        4·56

8. 24·51
    − 6·36
    ──────
      18·15

9. 19·63
    − 7·85
    ──────
      11·78

10. 17·29
    − 5·64
    ──────
      11·65

11. 21·64
    − 7·83
    ──────
      13·81

12. 15·83
    − 4·57
    ──────
      11·26

13. 23·75
    − 8·97
    ──────
      14·78

14. 18·34
    − 5·36
    ──────
      12·98

Rocket Answers may vary, but the answer is always in the format: ABBC, where A is one less than the value of the digits in the original 4-digit number. (If starting with 1111 the thousands digit in the answer will be 0.)

Page 71
Multiplying

1. 3 × [4 = 12 | 0·6 = 1·8]
    12·0
    + 1·8
    ──────
      13·8

2. 4 × [2 = 8 | 0·7 = 2·8]
      8·0
    + 2·8
    ──────
      10·8

3. 7 × [3 = 21 | 0·4 = 2·8]
      21·0
    +   2·8
    ──────
      23·8

4. 8 × [5 = 40 | 0·9 = 7·2]
      40·0
    +   7·2
    ──────
      47·2

5. 6 × [6 = 36 | 0·8 = 4·8]
      36·0
    +   4·8
    ──────
      40·8

6. 9 × [7 = 63 | 0·4 = 3·6]
      63·0
    +   3·6
    ──────
      66·6

7. 5 × [6 = 30 | 0·3 = 1·5]
      30·0
    +   1·5
    ──────
      31·5

8. 7 × [7 = 49 | 0·2 = 1·4]
      49·0
    +   1·4
    ──────
      50·4

9. 6 × [5 = 30 | 0·6 = 3·6]
      30·0
    +   3·6
    ──────
      33·6

10. 7 × [6 = 42 | 0·3 = 2·1]
      42·0
    +   2·1
    ──────
      44·1

11. 7 × [4 = 28 | 0·6 = 4·2]
      28·0
    +   4·2
    ──────
      32·2

12. 7 × [7 = 49 | 0·4 = 2·8]
      49·0
    +   2·8
    ──────
      51·8

13. 7 × [9 = 63 | 0·7 = 4·9]
      63·0
    +   4·9
    ──────
      67·9

14. 7 × [5 = 35 | 0·8 = 5·6]
      35·0
    +   5·6
    ──────
      40·6

15. 7 × [8 = 56 | 0·3 = 2·1]
      56·0
    +   2·1
    ──────
      58·1

16. 7 × [5 = 35 | 0·4 = 2·8]
      35·0
    +   2·8
    ──────
      37·8

17. 7 × [8 = 56 | 0·4 = 2·8]
      56·0
    +   2·8
    ──────
      58·8

18.

	5	0·6
7	35	4·2

```
  3 5 · 0
+     4 · 2
─────────
  3 9 · 2
```

19.

	3	0·2
7	21	1·4

```
  2 1 · 0
+     1 · 4
─────────
  2 2 · 4
```

Rocket Answers may vary. For example:
7 × 2·9 = 20·3

Page 72
Multiplying

1.

	6	0·3
4	24	1·2

```
  2 4 · 0
+     1 · 2
─────────
  2 5 · 2
```

2.

	7	0·4
6	42	2·4

```
  4 2 · 0
+     2 · 4
─────────
  4 4 · 4
```

3.

	3	0·9
7	21	6·3

```
  2 1 · 0
+     6 · 3
─────────
  2 7 · 3
```

4.

	5	0·8
8	40	6·4

```
  4 0 · 0
+     6 · 4
─────────
  4 6 · 4
```

5.

	8	0·7
3	24	2·1

```
  2 4 · 0
+     2 · 1
─────────
  2 6 · 1
```

6.

	7	0·3
6	42	1·8

```
  4 2 · 0
+     1 · 8
─────────
  4 3 · 8
```

7.

	4	0·3
6	24	1·8

```
  2 4 · 0
+     1 · 8
─────────
  2 5 · 8  cm
```

8. 4 × 6·8 cm = 27·2 cm
9. 7 × 3·8 cm = 26·6 cm
10. 8 × 4·7 cm = 37·6 cm
11. 6 × 5·2 cm = 31·2 cm
12. 9 × 3·4 cm = 30·6 cm
Rocket The stack could be made from seven tins of tuna.

Page 73
Multiplying

1. 7 × 4·6 = 32·2   7 × 4·0 = 28·0
                               7 × 0·6 = 4·2
                               7 × 4·6 = 32·2
2. 4 × 7·4 = 29·6
3. 3 × 8·6 = 25·8
4. 8 × 4·9 = 39·2
5. 6 × 5·7 = 34·2
6. 9 × 3·8 = 34·2
7. 7 × 6·4 = 44·8
8. 8 × 9·4 = 75·2
9. 6 × 7·9 = 47·4
10. 9 × 5·2 = 46·8
11. 7 × 3·6 = 25·2
12. 8 × 5·7 = 45·6
13. 6 × 4·2 kg = 25·2 kg
14. 4 × 2·7 kg = 10·8 kg
15. 7 × 3·8 kg = 26·6 kg
16. 8 × 1·6 kg = 12·8 kg
17. 7 × 2·4 kg = 16·8 kg
18. 5 × 6·8 kg = 34 kg
19. 8 × 4·9 kg = 39·2 kg
20. 3 × 5·7 kg = 17·1 kg
21. 9 × 3·3 kg = 29·7 kg
Rocket The largest answer you can make is 7·6 × 8 = 60·8; the smallest is 7·8 × 6 = 46·8.

Page 74
Multiplying

Children's methods may vary.

1. 9 × 4·7 = 42·3   9 × 4·0 = 36
                               9 × 0·7 = 6·3
                               9 × 4·7 = 42·3
                               42·3 ÷ 9 = 4·7
2. 8 × 3·4 = 27·2
3. 6 × 5·2 = 31·2
4. 7 × 8·6 = 60·2
5. 4 × 9·3 = 37·2
6. 5 × 4·3 = 21·5
7. 8 × 3·9 = 31·2
8. 6 × 7·6 = 45·6
9. 7 × 6·4 = 44·8
Rocket Regular triangle: perimeter = 4·7 cm × 3 = 14·1 cm
Square: perimeter = 4·7 cm × 4 = 18·8 cm
Regular pentagon: perimeter = 4·7 cm × 5 = 23·5 cm
Regular hexagon: perimeter = 4·7 cm × 6 = 28·2 cm
Regular heptagon: perimeter = 4·7 cm × 7 = 32·9 cm
Regular octagon: perimeter = 4·7 cm × 8 = 37·6 cm
and so on.
Estimates for questions **10–14** may vary.
10. 3·6 × 4 = 14·4; 2·8 × 9 = 25·2; 5·2 × 5 = 26; 4·3 × 7 = 30·1
11. 2·7 × 8 = 21·6; 5·8 × 4 = 23·2; 7·9 × 3 = 23·7; 4·2 × 6 = 25·2
12. 2·8 × 9 = 25·2; 9·2 × 3 = 27·6; 4·4 × 7 = 30·8; 6·3 × 5 = 31·5
13. 9·3 × 2 = 18·6; 4·9 × 4 = 19·6; 4·2 × 5 = 21; 2·7 × 8 = 21·6
14. 5·4 × 9 = 48·6; 7·3 × 7 = 51·1; 8·7 × 6 = 52·2; 6·6 × 8 = 52·8

Page 75
Multiplying

Children may show their working in various ways.

1. 30·1
2. 41·6
3. 14·4
4. 17·4
5. 57·6
6. 46·8
7. 11·6
8. 23·1
9. 23 or 23·0
10. 18·9
11. 14 or 14·0
12. 21·6
13. 19·8
14. 18·5
15. 17·2
16. 21·6 seconds
17. 22·4 seconds
18. 64·4 seconds
19. 32 seconds
20. 56·4 seconds
21. 26·1 seconds
22. 13·3 seconds
23. 28·2 seconds
24. 29·2 seconds
Rocket Answers will vary.

Page 76
Multiplying

Children may show their working in various ways.

1.

	4	0·5	0·06
3	12	1·5	0·18

```
   1 2 · 0
       1 · 5
+      0 · 1 8
─────────────
 £ 1 3 · 6 8
```

2. £14·72
3. £28·70
4. £69·76
5. £8·25
6. £47·10
7. £15·84
8. £26·16

Rocket Answers will vary.
9. 3 × 1·26 = 3·78
10. 4 × 2·57 = 10·28
11. 5 × 4·36 = 21·8
12. 8 × 7·42 = 59·36
13. 9 × 3·87 = 34·83
14. 4 × 8·64 = 34·56
15. 7 × 3·92 = 27·44
16. 6 × 4·38 = 26·28
17. 9 × 5·28 = 47·52

Page 77
Multiplying
Children may show their working in various ways.
1. 5 × 4·32 = 21·6   5 × 4 = 20
                       5 × 0·3 = 1·5
                       5 × 0·02 = 0·1
2. 6 × 3·78 = 22·68
3. 2 × 9·41 = 18·82
4. 3 × 6·75 = 20·25
5. 4 × 5·23 = 20·92
6. 7 × 2·85 = 19·95
7. 8 × 2·23 = 17·84
8. 9 × 1·84 = 16·56
9. 4 × 4·72 = 18·88

Lucy's answer is nearest to 20; Ben's answer is second nearest.
10. 12·96 cm
11. 22·8 cm
12. 45·84 cm
13. 27·84 cm
14. 26·82 cm
15. 61·47 cm
16. 52·02 cm
17. 54·72 cm

Rocket Triangle: 11·07 cm
Square: 14·76 cm
Pentagon: 18·45 cm
Hexagon: 22·14 cm
Heptagon: 25·83 cm
Octagon: 29·52 cm
Nonagon: 33·21 cm
Decagon: 36·9 cm

Page 78
Multiplying
1. 4·72
2. 3·84
3. 4·32
4. 6·89
5. 5·76
6. 7·58

Rocket Answers will vary.
7. Jim's fence is 7 m short; he needs to buy 4 more pieces.
8. £12·48
9. £11·72

Page 79
Dividing
Children's methods may vary.
1. 13·3
2. 18·4
3. 14·7
4. 13·2
5. 12·3
6. 15·1
7. 17·2 km
8. 14·7 km
9. 11·3 km
10. 23·6 km
11. 22·7 km
12. 13·9 km
13. 12·7 km
14. 26·8 km
15. 18·8 km

Rocket
7. 7·8 km
8. 18·6 km approx
9. 13·7 km
10. 9·7 km approx
11. 2·3 km
12. 19·4 km approx
13. 4 km approx
14. 6·5 km approx
15. 6·2 km

Page 80
Dividing
Children's methods may vary.
1.
```
    2 8 · 2 g
3 ) 8 4 · 6 g
  - 6 0        (20) × 3
    2 4 · 6
  - 2 4        (8) × 3
      0 · 6
    - 0 · 6    (0·2) × 3
      0
```
2. 13·6 g
3. 19·8 g
4. 17·7 g
5. 12·9 g
6. 8·8 g
7. 22·7 g
8. 29·4 g
9. 22·5 g

Answers will vary, but will include three of the following calculations:
1. 28·2 × 3 = 84·6 g
2. 13·6 × 6 = 81·6 g
3. 19·8 × 4 = 79·2 g
4. 17·7 × 5 = 88·5 g
5. 12·9 × 7 = 90·3 g
6. 8·8 × 4 = 35·2 g
7. 22·7 × 4 = 90·8 g
8. 29·4 × 3 = 88·2 g
9. 22·5 × 3 = 67·6 g

Rocket No written answers.
10. 14·7
11. 23·6
12. 12·2
13. 11·8
14. 16·4
15. 32·3
16. 21·6
17. 13·7
18. 23·9

Page 81
Dividing
Children's methods may vary.
1. 0·7
2. 0·9
3. 0·8
4. 0·8
5. 16·5
6. 5·9
7. 8·2
8. 5·8
9. 18·5
10. 7·9
11. 5·2
12. 9·9
13. 16·4
14. 5·9
15. 7·9
16. 4·6

Rocket Answers will vary.
17. 76·3
18. 76·5
19. 208·7
20. 103·8
21. 142·7
22. 26·8
23. 34·5
24. 70·7
25. 62·5

Page 82
Dividing
Children's methods may vary.
1.
```
    5 · 2 4
  - 4          (1) × 4
    1 · 2 4
    1 · 2      (0·3) × 4
    0 · 0 4
    0 · 0 4    (0·01) × 4
    0
```
5·24 ÷ 4 = 1·31
2. 3·15 ÷ 5 = 0·63
3. 4·16 ÷ 4 = 1·04
4. 8·24 ÷ 2 = 4·12
5. 12·39 ÷ 3 = 4·13
6. 7·68 ÷ 4 = 1·92
7. 14·77 ÷ 7 = 2·11
8. 7·56 ÷ 6 = 1·26
9. 5·45 ÷ 5 = 1·09
10. 6·28 ÷ 4 = 1·57
11. 2·68 ÷ 4 = 0·67
12. 4·68 ÷ 2 = 2·34

Natalie's answer is closest to 1.
Rocket Highest answer: 86·5 ÷ 2 = 43·25; lowest answer: 2·56 ÷ 8 = 0·32.
Various answers will come close to 1. The closest is 5·82 ÷ 6 = 0·97.

Page 83
Dividing
Children's methods may vary.
1.
```
    7 · 2 8 m
  - 4          = (1) × 4
    3 · 2 8
    3 · 2 0    = (0·8) × 4
    0 · 0 8
    0 · 0 8    = (0·02) × 4
    0
```
7·28 m ÷ 4 = 1·82 m
2. 8·22 m ÷ 3 = 2·74 m
3. 9·72 m ÷ 9 = 1·08 m
4. 6·95 m ÷ 5 = 1·39 m

Rocket Answers will vary. Children can subtract a length for the shorter side so that an amount exactly divisible by 3 is left for the three longer sides. One possible answer is that the three equal sides are 2·14 m each, and the shorter side is 2 m. Or the shorter side could be 0·32 m, leaving 8·1 m, so the three equal sides are 2·7 m each.

5. 27·34 m
6. 18·46 m
7. 13·64 m
8. 12·82 m
9. 32·14 m
10. 11·78 m
11. 21·23 m
12. 12·44 m
13. 26·46 m

Page 84
Dividing

Children's methods may vary.

1.
```
   £ 3 3 · 3 6
 -     3 2      (8)   × 4
       1 · 3 6
       1 · 2 0  (0·3) × 4
       0 · 1 6
 -     0 · 1 6  (0·04) × 4
             0
```
£33·36 ÷ 4 = £8·34

2. £6·28
3. £7·46
4. £9·53
5. £6·72
6. £8·47
7. 856·8 ÷ 40 = 85·68 ÷ 4 = 21·42
8. 883·8 ÷ 60 = 88·38 ÷ 6 = 14·73
9. 97·53 ÷ 30 = 9·753 ÷ 3 = 3·251
10. 886·9 ÷ 70 = 88·69 ÷ 7 = 12·67
11. 942·4 ÷ 80 = 94·24 ÷ 8 = 11·78
12. 975·6 ÷ 90 = 97·56 ÷ 9 = 10·84

Rocket The trick is to multiply both parts by 10. So 18·36 ÷ 0·3 = 183·6 ÷ 3 = 61·2; and 24·84 ÷ 0·04 = 2484 ÷ 4 = 621.

Page 85
Percentages of amounts

1. Mashed banana : 37·5 ml
   Pineapple juice: 75 ml
   Mashed mango: 150 ml
   Orange juice: 487·5 ml

Rocket Mashed banana: 75 ml, 5%
Pineapple juice: 150 ml, 10%
Mashed mango: 300 ml, 20%
Orange juice: 975 ml, 65%

2. Crushed cherries: 2·5 ml
   Mashed banana: 5 ml
   Orange juice: 12·5 ml
   Apple juice: 17·5 ml
   Crushed raspberries: 25 ml
   Crushed strawberries: 37·5 ml
   Bramble juice: 150 ml

Rocket Answers will vary.

Page 86
Percentages of amounts

1. £90
2.

Name	Percentage	Number of points scored
Douglas	50%	140
Ella	25%	70
John	15%	42
Kirsten	10%	28

Rocket Girls
Protein: 190–570 calories
Carbohydrates: 855–1235 calories
Fats: 475–665 calories

Boys
Protein: 240–720 calories
Carbohydrates: 1080–1560 calories
Fats: 600–840 calories

Page 87
Percentages of amounts

1. 15 ml
2. 37·5 ml
3. 225 ml
4. 13·5 g
5. 36 g
6. 63 g
7. 90 ml
8. 337·5 ml
9. 540 ml
10. 608 ml
11. 228 ml
12. 1064 ml

Rocket Each day: 70 ml; each week: 490 ml.

Page 88
Percentage increase

1. 250 g
2. 495 g
3. 1020 g
4. 728 g
5. 735 g
6. 1410 g
7. 910 g
8. 1071 g
9. Biscuits: £8·74
   Scones: £7·82
   Tray bakes: £17·71
   Sponge cake: £14·72

10.

Name	Event	Previous record	Percentage increase	New record
Jamil	High jump	1·36 m	10%	1·496 m
Hilary	Long jump	2·25 m	5%	2·3625 m
Katie	Shot putt	5·35 m	20%	6·42 m

Page 89
Percentage decrease

1. £450
2. £405
3. £384
4. £252
5. £750·50
6. £482·50
7. £82·80
8. £83·60

9.

Type of Ticket	Previous price	Percentage decrease	New price
Adult	£275	10%	£247·50
Child U12	£145	75%	£36·25
Youth U18	£165	20%	£132
OAP	£150	30%	£105
Family	£635	40%	£381

Page 90
Percentage change

1. £4875
2. £4005
3. £2784
4. £3052
5. £1795·50
6. £5575·50
7. £2030·40
8. £7310
9. Average high °C:
   May: 15·45
   Aug: 17·64
   Nov: 8·32
   Rainfall mm:
   March: 78·44
   July: 41·5
   December: 69·75

Rocket £110·25

Page 91
Percentage calculations

1.

Name	Spelling	Maths	General knowledge
Simona	$\frac{6}{10}$ = 60%	$\frac{14}{20}$ = 70%	$\frac{20}{40}$ = 50%
Katie	$\frac{7}{10}$ = 70%	$\frac{15}{20}$ = 75%	$\frac{10}{40}$ = 25%
Wai-Sen	$\frac{10}{10}$ = 100%	$\frac{12}{20}$ = 60%	$\frac{25}{40}$ = 62·5%
Faye	$\frac{3}{10}$ = 30%	$\frac{8}{20}$ = 40%	$\frac{26}{40}$ = 65%
Eshveer	$\frac{5}{10}$ = 50%	$\frac{16}{20}$ = 80%	$\frac{34}{40}$ = 85%
James	$\frac{9}{10}$ = 90%	$\frac{13}{20}$ = 65%	$\frac{38}{40}$ = 95%
Catherine	$\frac{8}{10}$ = 80%	$\frac{17}{20}$ = 85%	$\frac{16}{40}$ = 40%
Andrew	$\frac{2}{10}$ = 20%	$\frac{11}{20}$ = 55%	$\frac{28}{40}$ = 70%

2. Simona did best in maths.
   Katie did best in maths.
   Wai-Sen did best in spelling.
   Faye did best in general knowledge.
   Eshveer did best in general knowledge.
   James did best in general knowledge.
   Catherine did best in maths.
   Andrew did best in general knowledge.

Rocket Increasing an amount by 10% is the same as adding on an extra tenth. Multiplying the amount by 1 would not change the amount, but multiplying by 1·1 has the effect of increasing the amount by a tenth.
45 × 1·1 = 45 + a tenth of 45 = 45 + 4·5 = 49.5

Page 92
Percentage calculations

1. $\frac{1}{2}$ = 50%
2. $\frac{2}{10}$ = 20%
3. $\frac{2}{5}$ = 40%
4. $\frac{3}{4}$ = 75%
5. $\frac{30}{60}$ = 50%
6. $\frac{3}{12}$ = 25%
7. $\frac{6}{8}$ = 75%
8. $\frac{9}{12}$ = 75%
9. 60%
10. 50%

11.

Colour	Number of children	Percentage of the class
Red	8	40%
Purple	4	20%
Blue	6	30%
Pink	2	10%

Rocket Answers will vary.

Page 93
Percentage calculations

1. Wei: 62·5%
   Tom: 25%
   Abraham: 12·5%
2. £400 = 50% of total
3. £600 = 75% of total
4. £800 = 100% of total
5. Wei: 20% of total
   Tom: 40% of total
   Abraham: 40% of total
6. Answers will vary.

Rocket 125%

Page 94
Word problems

There are 3 blue sweets, 12 red sweets, 9 yellow sweets and 6 green sweets.

1. There are most of the red sweets.
2. There are fewest of the blue sweets.

Rocket Answers will vary.

3. Answers will vary. One method of comparing the information is to increase the Bon biscuit values by 50% to find what they would be if both biscuits = 15 g.
4. Answers will vary depending on the method that the children are using to compare the nutritional information of the biscuits, and they do not have to draw a table.

Nutritional information	In a 10 g Bon biscuit	Per 15 g Bon biscuit	Nutritional information	In a 15 g Oaty oat
Protein	1·1 g	1·65 g	Protein	0·6 g
Carbohydrate	8·3 g	12·45 g	Carbohydrate	9·6 g
Fat	3·1 g	4·65 g	Fat	4·7 g
Fibre	0·6 g	0·9 g	Fibre	0·9 g
Salt	0·1 g	0·15 g	Salt	0·3 g

Answers will vary but may include:
The Oaty oat biscuit has less carbohydrate than the Bon biscuit, per 15 g: 9·6 g compared to 12·45 g.
The Bon biscuit has slightly less fat than the Oaty oat biscuit, per 15 g: 4·65 g compared to 4·7 g.
The two biscuits have exactly the same amount of fibre per 15 g, 0·9 g.
The Bon biscuit has 0·15 g of salt, per 15 g, exactly half as much salt as the Oaty oat biscuit.

Page 95
Calculation investigations

1. 64
2. Answers will vary, for example: 19 ÷ 4 = 4 r 3.
3. Answers will vary, for example: 20 ÷ 8 = 2$\frac{1}{2}$.
4. Answers will vary, for example: 102 ÷ 30 = 3·4.
5. Answers will vary, but could include a question where a whole number is needed, for example: 17 children are split into teams of 5, how many teams are there? This answer is rounded up to account for every child.
6. Answers will vary, but could include: A teacher has £51 to spend on a school outing for 15 children. She has to spend the same amount on each child. How much would that be?
7. Answers will vary, but could include: A garden measures 34 m². It has one side that is 10 m long. What is the length of the other side rounded to the nearest half metre?
8. Methods for calculating this answer will vary. The answer should come to: 3·12.

Fractions, Decimals and Percentages PPMs

PPM 76
Fractions of a shape
1. $\frac{1}{2}$
2. $\frac{1}{6}$
3. $\frac{1}{5}$
4. $\frac{1}{2}$
5. $\frac{1}{4}$
6. $\frac{1}{10}$
7. $\frac{1}{3}$

PPM 77
Fractions on a number line
1. $\frac{1}{2}$
2. $\frac{1}{5}$
3. $\frac{1}{4}$
4. $\frac{1}{8}$
5. $\frac{1}{10}$
6. $\frac{1}{6}$

PPM 78
Fractions of a shape
1. $\frac{3}{4}$ shaded, $\frac{1}{4}$ not shaded
2. $\frac{5}{6}$ shaded, $\frac{1}{6}$ not shaded
3. $\frac{1}{3}$ shaded, $\frac{2}{3}$ not shaded
4. $\frac{7}{10}$ shaded, $\frac{3}{10}$ not shaded
5. $\frac{3}{5}$ shaded, $\frac{2}{5}$ not shaded
6. $\frac{1}{12}$ shaded, $\frac{11}{12}$ not shaded

PPM 79
Fractions on a number line
1. $\frac{3}{4}$
2. $\frac{2}{5}$
3. $\frac{7}{8}$
4. $\frac{3}{10}$
5. $\frac{4}{6}$

PPM 80
Comparing fractions
1.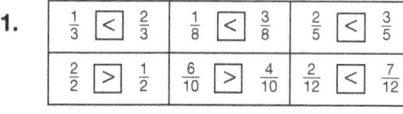
2. $\frac{1}{10}, \frac{1}{8}, \frac{1}{6}, \frac{1}{5}, \frac{1}{4}, \frac{1}{3}, \frac{1}{2}$
3. $\frac{1}{2}, \frac{1}{5}, \frac{1}{6}, \frac{1}{8}, \frac{1}{8}, \frac{1}{10}$
4. one tenth, one quarter, one third

PPM 81
Comparing fractions
1.

$\frac{1}{3}$ < $\frac{2}{3}$	$\frac{1}{8}$ < $\frac{3}{8}$	$\frac{2}{5}$ < $\frac{3}{5}$
$\frac{2}{2}$ > $\frac{1}{2}$	$\frac{6}{10}$ > $\frac{4}{10}$	$\frac{2}{12}$ < $\frac{7}{12}$

2. $\frac{3}{10}, \frac{7}{10}, \frac{8}{10},$
   $\frac{1}{5}, \frac{3}{5}, \frac{4}{5},$
   $\frac{1}{4}, \frac{2}{4}, \frac{3}{4}$
3. $\frac{6}{6}, \frac{3}{3}, \frac{6}{8}, \frac{3}{8}, \frac{2}{8}, \frac{1}{6}$ OR $\frac{3}{3}, \frac{6}{6}, \frac{6}{8}, \frac{3}{8}, \frac{2}{8}, \frac{1}{6}$
4. two eighths, four eighths, eight eighths

PPM 82
Comparing fractions
1.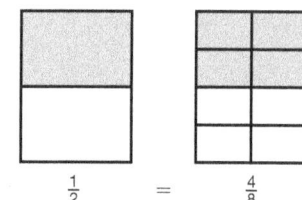
2. $\frac{2}{4} = \frac{1}{2}$
3. $\frac{3}{4} = \frac{6}{8}$
4. Answers will vary.

PPM 83
Equivalent fractions
1.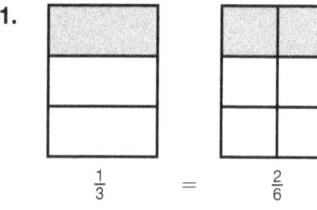
2.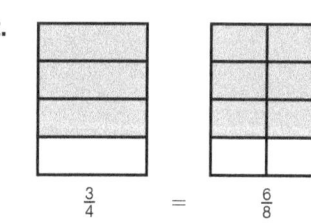
3.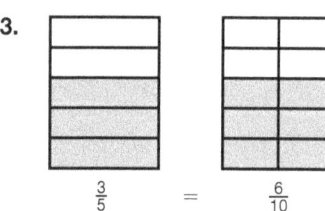
4.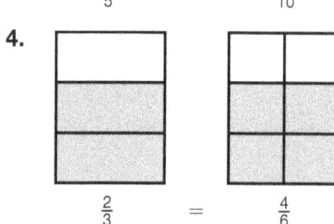
5.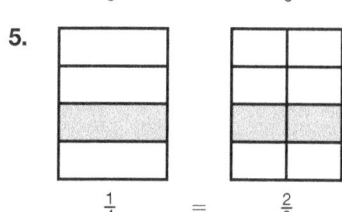

PPM 84
Mixed numbers to improper fractions
1. $\frac{13}{4}$ 2. $\frac{8}{3}$
3. $\frac{8}{5}$ 4. $\frac{30}{7}$
5. $\frac{15}{2}$ 6. $\frac{33}{8}$
7. $\frac{37}{10}$ 8. $\frac{27}{5}$
9. $\frac{17}{6}$ 10. $\frac{27}{8}$
11. $\frac{13}{7}$ 12. $\frac{49}{10}$
13. $\frac{29}{9}$ 14. $\frac{16}{3}$
15. $\frac{31}{4}$

PPM85
Improper fractions to mixed numbers
1. $2\frac{2}{3}$ 2. $4\frac{1}{2}$
3. $2\frac{3}{5}$ 4. $5\frac{3}{4}$
5. $3\frac{1}{6}$ 6. $7\frac{7}{10}$
7. $2\frac{7}{8}$ 8. $7\frac{4}{7}$
9. $3\frac{1}{9}$ 10. $7\frac{3}{4}$
11. $8\frac{2}{3}$ 12. $8\frac{2}{5}$
13. $5\frac{8}{11}$ 14. $5\frac{17}{20}$

PPM 86
Mixed numbers on a number line
1. $2\frac{1}{8}, 2\frac{5}{8}, 2\frac{7}{8}$
2. $4\frac{2}{5}, 4\frac{4}{5}$
3. $6\frac{1}{6}, 6\frac{3}{6}, 6\frac{5}{6}$
4. $4\frac{3}{10}, 4\frac{6}{10}, 4\frac{9}{10}$
5. $1\frac{1}{12}, 1\frac{5}{12}, 1\frac{7}{12}, 1\frac{11}{12}$

PPM 87
Creating equivalent fractions
1. $\frac{2}{6}$ 2. $\frac{2}{4}$
3. $\frac{4}{6}$ 4. $\frac{8}{8}$
5. $\frac{8}{16}$ 6. $\frac{6}{12}$
7. $\frac{3}{4}$ 8. $\frac{1}{2}$
9. $\frac{9}{12}$ 10. $\frac{2}{4}$
11. $\frac{3}{4}$ 12. $\frac{1}{4}$
13. $\frac{12}{16}$ 14. $\frac{6}{12}$
15. $\frac{4}{12}$ 16. $\frac{2}{4}$
17. $\frac{6}{6}$ 18. $\frac{4}{10}$

PPM 88
Equivalent fractions
1. $\frac{2}{6}$ 2. $\frac{6}{8}$
3. $\frac{8}{10}$ 4. $\frac{14}{20}$
5. $\frac{3}{6}$ 6. $\frac{3}{12}$
7. $\frac{6}{9}$ 8. $\frac{8}{10}$

9. $\frac{2}{3}$
10. $\frac{3}{4}$
11. $\frac{15}{35}$
12. $\frac{12}{27}$
13. $\frac{12}{20}$
14. $\frac{14}{21}$
15. $\frac{35}{40}$

PPM 89
Ordering fractions

1. $\frac{9}{12} > \frac{8}{12}$
2. $\frac{4}{10} < \frac{5}{10}$
3. $\frac{16}{20} > \frac{15}{20}$
4. $\frac{7}{10} > \frac{6}{10}$
5. $\frac{10}{15} < \frac{12}{15}$
6. $\frac{9}{12} < \frac{10}{12}$
7. $\frac{20}{24} < \frac{21}{24}$
8. $\frac{16}{18} > \frac{15}{18}$

PPM 90
Ordering fractions

1. $\frac{3}{4} > \frac{5}{8}$
2. $\frac{5}{6} > \frac{2}{3}$
3. $\frac{1}{2} < \frac{7}{12}$
4. $\frac{11}{12} > \frac{5}{6}$
5. $\frac{7}{20} > \frac{3}{10}$
6. $\frac{4}{5} = \frac{8}{10}$
7. $\frac{11}{20} < \frac{3}{5}$
8. $\frac{1}{4} < \frac{5}{16}$
9. $\frac{7}{8} = \frac{14}{16}$
10. $\frac{2}{3} > \frac{7}{12}$
11. $\frac{3}{4} < \frac{17}{20}$
12. $\frac{5}{8} < \frac{11}{16}$
13. $\frac{3}{4} > \frac{2}{3}$
14. $\frac{8}{12} = \frac{2}{3}$
15. $\frac{4}{5} > \frac{3}{4}$
16. $\frac{3}{8} < \frac{5}{6}$

PPM 91
Ordering fractions

Answers will vary.

PPM 92
Fractions of money

1. 9p
2. 7p
3. 8p
4. 5p
5. 11p
6. 7p
7. 6p
8. 4p
9. 7p
10. 3p
11. 9p
12. 8p
13. 9p
14. 11p
15. 8p
16. 9p

PPM 93
Fractions of weights

1. 8 kg
2. 6 kg
3. 8 kg
4. 10 kg
5. 9 kg
6. 6 kg
7. 24 kg
8. 35 kg
9. 15 kg
10. 20 kg
11. 20 kg
12. 15 kg
13. 8 kg
14. 9 kg
15. Answers will vary.

PPM 94
Hundredths

1. A: 5·18
   B: 5·36
   C: 5·45
   D: 5·54
   E: 5·71
   F: 5·87
2. G: 7·08
   H: 7·31
   I: 7·40
   J: 7·54
   K: 7·72
   L: 7·94
3. M: 13·14
   N: 13·31
   O: 13·49
   P: 13·65
   Q: 13·82
   R: 13·96

PPM 95
Hundredths

Answers will vary.

PPM 96
Fractions and decimals

1. 50 squares

   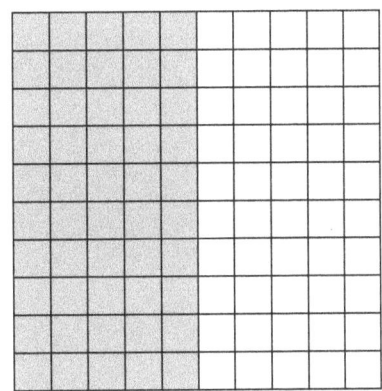

   Decimal 0·5   Fraction $\frac{1}{2}$

2. 25 squares

   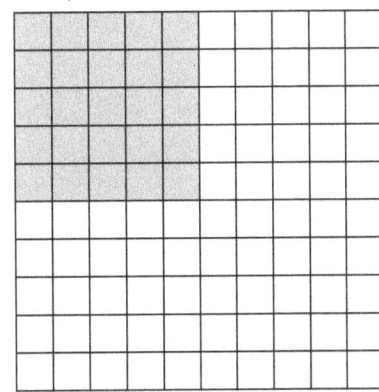

   Decimal 0·25   Fraction $\frac{1}{4}$

3. 75 squares

   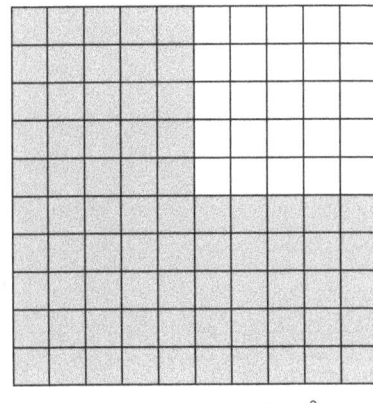

   Decimal 0·75   Fraction $\frac{3}{4}$

4. 20 squares

   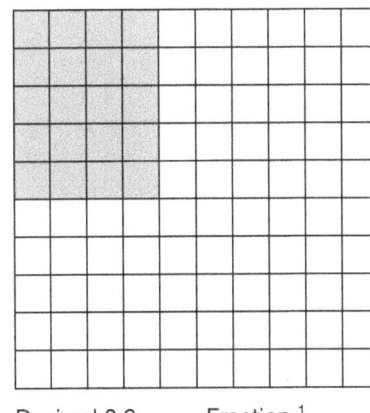

   Decimal 0·2   Fraction $\frac{1}{5}$

5. 60 squares

   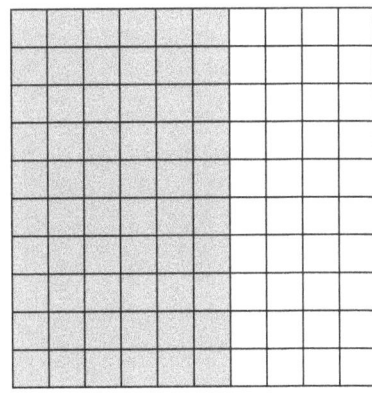

   Decimal 0·6   Fraction $\frac{3}{5}$

6. 30 squares

   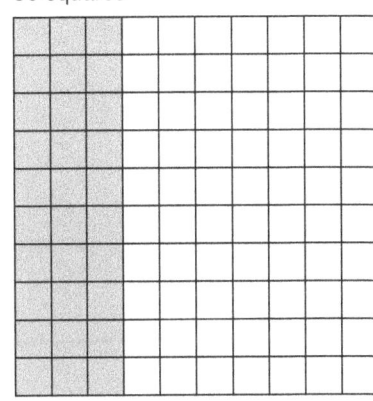

   Decimal 0·3   Fraction $\frac{3}{10}$

PPM 97
Fractions and decimals

1.

Fraction in simplest form	Decimal Fraction	Number of hundredths
$\frac{1}{2}$	0·5	50
$\frac{1}{4}$	0·25	25
$\frac{4}{10}$	0·4	40
$\frac{3}{4}$	0·75	75
$\frac{1}{10}$	0·1	10
$\frac{4}{5}$	0·8	80
$\frac{7}{10}$	0·7	70
$\frac{3}{10}$	0·3	30
$\frac{3}{5}$	0·6	60
$1\frac{1}{2}$	1·5	150
$2\frac{1}{4}$	2·25	225
$4\frac{4}{5}$	4·8	480

2. Answers will vary.

PPM 98
Fractions and decimals

1. $\frac{3}{5} = 0·6$ or $\frac{3}{6} = 0·5$
2. $\frac{8}{5} = 1·6$
3. $\frac{9}{10} = 0·9$
4. $\frac{9}{2} = 4·5$
5. $\frac{13}{5} = 2·6$ or $\frac{13}{2} = 6·5$
6. $\frac{14}{10} = 1·4$
7. $\frac{31}{5} = 6·2$
8. $\frac{8}{20} = 0·4$
9. $\frac{14}{20} = 0·7$
10. $\frac{60}{40} = 1·5$

PPM 99
Ordering decimals

1. [number line 1·0 to 2·0 with arrows]
2. [number line 6·0 to 7·0 with arrows]
3. [number line 3·0 to 4·0 with arrows]
4. [number line 9·0 to 10·0 with arrows]
5. [number line 5·0 to 6·0 with arrows]
6. [number line 1·0 to 2·0 with arrows]
7. 145 cm, 2·5 m, 2·51 m, 3·05, 3·2 m, 5·71 m

PPM 100
Ordering decimals

1. 5·4 > 5·3
2. 5·23 < 5·26
3. 5·25 < 5·35
4. 5·35 < 5·53
5. 5·2 > 5
6. 5·25 < 5·5
7. 5·3 > 5·27
8. 5·46 < 5·5
9. 5·29 < 5·3
10. 5·1 > 5·09
11. 5·2 < 5·21
12. 5·34 < 5·43
13. 5·15 < 5·51
14. 5·21 < 5·3
15. $5\frac{3}{10} = 5·3$
16. $5\frac{17}{100} > 5·15$
17. $5·2 < 5\frac{21}{100}$
18. $5·35 > 5\frac{3}{10}$
19. $5·4 > 5\frac{39}{100}$
20. $5·06 < 5\frac{1}{10}$

PPM 101
Rounding to the nearest tenth

1. 7·24
2. 4·87
3. 2·47 or 2·48
4. 8·72 or 8·74
5. 4·72
6. 7·48
7. 8·27
8. 2·87
9. 7·82 or 7·84
10. 8·24
11. 4·82
12. 2·78 or 2·84
13. 8·47
14. 7·42
15. 2·74
16. 4·27 or 4·28
17. 7·28
18. 8·42

PPM 102
Rounding

1. 7·34, 7·39, 7·43 or 7·49
2. 3·47 or 3·49
3. 7·93 or 7·94
4. 4·73, 4·93, 4·97
5. 3·74, 3·79, 3·94 or 3·97
6. 9·34, 9·37, 9·43 or 9·47
7. 9·73 or 9·74
8. 6·13, 6·18, 6·31 or 6·38
9. 3·61, 3·68, 3·81 or 3·86
10. 1·36 or 1·38
11. 8·61 or 8·63
12. 8·13, 8·16, 8·31 or 8·36
13. 1·63, 1·68, 1·83 or 1·86
14. 3·16 or 3·18
15. 6·81 or 6·83

PPM 103
Multiplying by 10, 100 and 1000

1.

Number	×10	×100	×1000
3·8	38	380	3800
5·6	56	560	5600
6·3	63	630	6300
4·27	42·7	427	4270
6·53	65·3	653	6530
7·42	74·2	742	7420
6·85	68·5	685	6850
13·08	130·8	1308	13 080
12·35	123·5	1235	12 350
0·06	0·6	6	60
2·4	24	240	2400
0·02	0·2	2	20
50·09	500·9	5009	50 090

2. Answers will vary.

PPM 104
Dividing by 10 and 100

1. 8
2. $7\frac{1}{10}$ or 7·1
3. $\frac{46}{100}, \frac{23}{50}$ or 0·46
4. $\frac{93}{100}$ or 0·93
5. 47
6. $52\frac{6}{10}$ or 52·6
7. 34
8. 27
9. 81
10. 730
11. $\frac{19}{100}$ or 0·19
12. 49
13. $\frac{4}{100}, \frac{2}{50}, \frac{1}{25}$ or 0·04
14. $26\frac{5}{10}$ or 26·5
15. 431
16. 9
17. Answers will vary.

PPM 105
Percentages

Children's shading methods may vary.

1.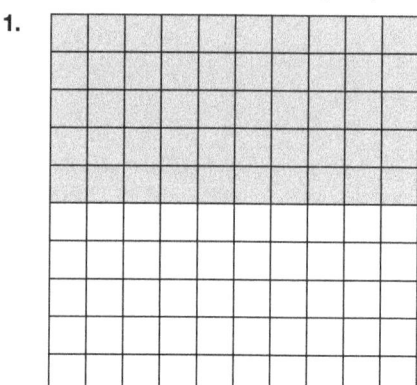

$\frac{1}{2} = \frac{50}{100} = 50\%$

2.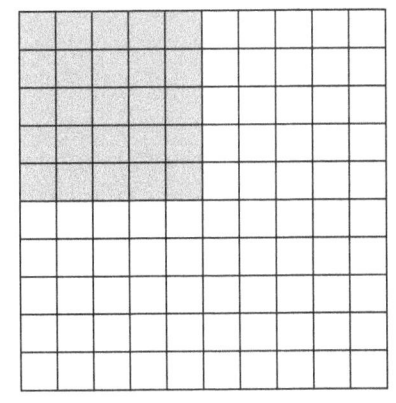
$\frac{1}{4} = \frac{25}{100} = 25\%$

3.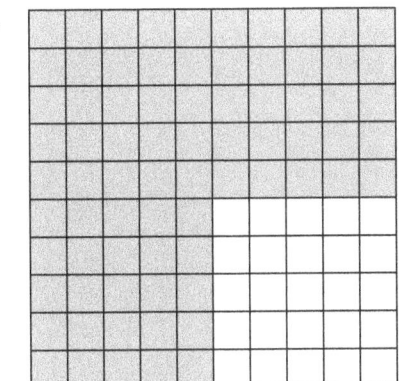
$\frac{3}{4} = \frac{75}{100} = 75\%$

4.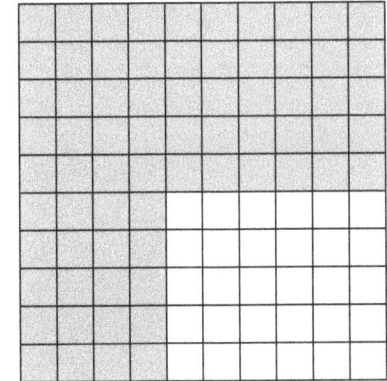
$\frac{7}{10} = \frac{70}{100} = 70\%$

5.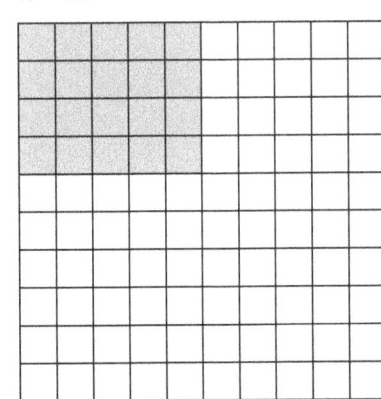
$\frac{1}{5} = \frac{20}{100} = 20\%$

6.
$\frac{4}{5} = \frac{80}{100} = 80\%$

7.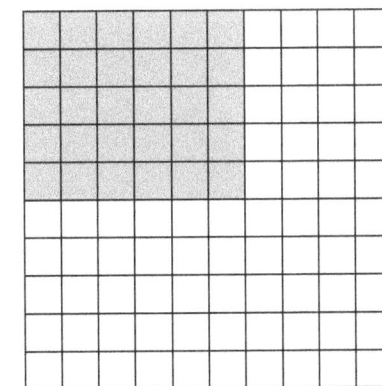
$\frac{3}{10} = \frac{30}{100} = 30\%$

8.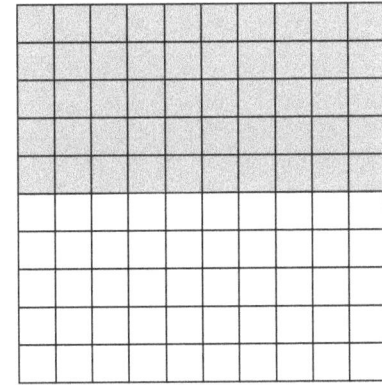
$\frac{10}{20} = \frac{50}{100} = 50\%$

9.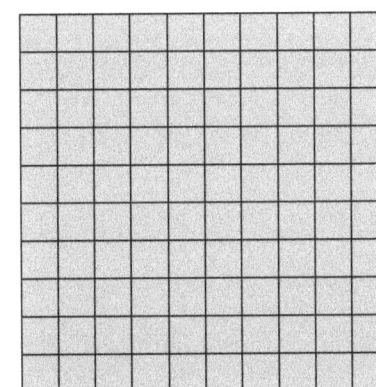
$\frac{10}{10} = \frac{100}{100} = 100\%$

PPM 106
Fractions and decimals as percentages

1. 30%
2. 90%
3. 11%
4. 25%
5. 50%
6. 35%
7. 60%
8. 75%
9. 74%
10. 20%
11. 20%
12. 10%
13. 2%
14. 80%
15. 50%
16. 25%
17. 75%
18. 20%
19. 98%
20. 99%
21. Answers will vary.

PPM 107
Percentages

1. £8
2. £4
3. £60
4. £40
5. £25
6. £12
7. £11
8. £15
9. £150
10. £50
11. £30
12. £24
13. £30
14. £52·50
15. £32
16. £45
17. £0·80
18. £1·80
19. £3
20. £1·20
21. Answers will vary.

PPM 108
Answering with fractions

1. $9\frac{1}{3}$
2. $23\frac{1}{2}$
3. $6\frac{3}{4}$
4. $7\frac{3}{7}$
5. $4\frac{5}{6}$
6. $7\frac{1}{3}$
7. $8\frac{3}{5}$
8. $4\frac{3}{4}$
9. $16\frac{1}{2}$
10. $5\frac{1}{3}$
11. $7\frac{1}{8}$
12. $6\frac{1}{3}$
13. $9\frac{3}{4}$
14. $5\frac{1}{7}$
15. $5\frac{2}{3}$
16. $5\frac{3}{5}$
17. $9\frac{1}{6}$
18. $6\frac{3}{7}$

PPM 109
Answering with decimals

1. N
2. C
3. D
4. B
5. H
6. F
7. J
8. O
9. A
10. E
11. I
12. L
13. P
14. K
15. R
16. Q
17. M
18. G

PPM 110
Fractions and decimal fractions

1.

Fraction	Means	Decimal answer on a calculator
$\frac{6}{10}$	6 ÷ 10	0·6
$\frac{4}{5}$	4 ÷ 5	0·8
$\frac{1}{2}$	1 ÷ 2	0·5
$\frac{3}{4}$	3 ÷ 4	0·75
$\frac{2}{5}$	2 ÷ 5	0·4
$\frac{15}{20}$	15 ÷ 20	0·75
$\frac{1}{8}$	1 ÷ 8	0·125
$\frac{3}{8}$	3 ÷ 8	0·375

Answers will vary in the bottom four rows.

2. Discussion, but children should reach the following conclusion: $\frac{1}{3}$, 1 ÷ 3, 0·333333.

PPM 111
Adding decimals

1.

+	3·1	2·5	1·9	4·8
5·6	8·7	8·1	7·5	10·4
7·2	10·3	9·7	9·1	12·0
1·7	4·8	4·2	3·6	6·5
2·9	6·0	5·4	4·8	7·7
4·5	7·6	7·0	6·4	9·3
1·3	4·4	3·8	3·2	6·1
2·7	5·8	5·2	4·6	7·5
5·8	8·9	8·3	7·7	10·6

2. Answers will vary.

PPM 112
Adding decimals

1. ⑦
   ```
     4·6 2
   + 1·7 5
     6·3 7
   ```
2. 12·79
3. 14·65
4. 6·45
5. 10·10 or 10·1
6. 13·82
7. 17·91
8. 6·40 or 6·4
9. 9·03
10. 17·29
11. 21·03
12. 10·54
13. Answers will vary.

PPM 113
Subtracting decimals

1. ⑤
   ```
     8·7 6
   - 3·5 2
     5·2 4
   ```
2. 4·11
3. 5·57
4. 5·26
5. 5·57
6. 1·77
7. 1·56
8. 4·30 or 4·3
9. 4·79
10. 2·25
11. 1·86
12. 1·17
13. Answers will vary.

PPM 114
Subtracting decimals

1. ②
   ```
     5·2 7
   - 3·1 4
     2·1 3
   ```
2. 4·47
3. 3·33
4. 5·35
5. 5·25
6. 3·44
7. 2·31
8. 2·83
9. 1·38
10. 1·09
11. 1·65
12. 2·13
13. Answers will vary.

PPM 115
Percentages of an amount

1.

Amount	10%	1%	5%	20%
380	38	3·8	19	76
470	47	4·7	23·5	94
530	53	5·3	26·5	106
680	68	6·8	34	136
920	92	9·2	46	184
1280	128	12·8	64	256
4760	476	47·6	238	952
2540	254	25·4	127	508
3690	369	36·9	184·5	738
4780	478	47·8	239	956
6590	659	65·9	329·5	1318
250	25	2·5	12·5	50
420	42	4·2	21	84
370	37	3·7	18·5	74
240	24	2·4	12	48
775	77·5	7·75	38·75	155

2. Answers will vary.

PPM 116
Percentages of an amount

1.

Amount	5%	10%	15%	25%
38	1·9	3·8	5·7	9·5
570	28·5	57	85·5	142·5
520	26	52	78	130
78	3·9	7·8	11·7	19·5
970	48·5	97	145·5	242·5
1680	84	168	252	420
4360	218	436	654	1090
2040	102	204	306	510
3620	181	362	543	905
8780	439	878	1317	2195
6490	324·5	649	973·5	1622·5
960	48	96	144	240
3950	197·5	395	592·5	987·5
150	7·5	15	22·5	37·5
640	32	64	96	160
3576	178·8	357·6	536·4	894

2. Answers will vary.

PPM 117
Half-price sale

1. DVD
2. Trainers, sunglasses and games console.
3. MP3 player and computer mouse.

PPM 118
Hamadi's camels

1. The reason that Sharifa's solution works is that the three fractions, $\frac{1}{2}$, $\frac{1}{4}$ and $\frac{1}{8}$, do not add up to 1 (they add up to $\frac{7}{8}$), so they do not account for the whole group of camels.
   Although it seems that each child ends up with the correct fraction of the camels, this is not quite true. Hamadi intended them to end up with fractions of 7:
   Neema: $\frac{1}{2}$ of 7 = 3·5
   Rashidi: $\frac{1}{4}$ of 7 = 1·75
   Asim: $\frac{1}{8}$ of 7 = 0·875
   What they end up with are fractions of 8:
   Neema: $\frac{1}{2}$ of 8 = 4
   Rashidi: $\frac{1}{4}$ of 8 = 2
   Asim: $\frac{1}{8}$ of 8 = 1
2. Answers will vary.

Fractions, Decimals and Percentages APMs

APM 356
Equivalent fractions

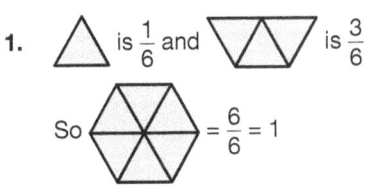

1. △ is $\frac{1}{6}$ and ▽▽ is $\frac{3}{6}$
   So ⬡ = $\frac{6}{6}$ = 1

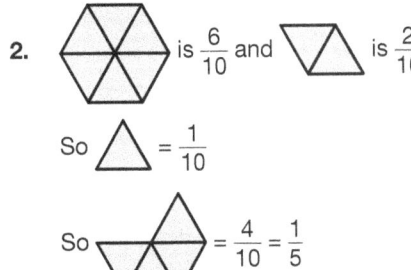

2. ⬡ is $\frac{6}{10}$ and △△ is $\frac{2}{10}$
   So △ = $\frac{1}{10}$
   So △△△△ = $\frac{4}{10}$ = $\frac{1}{5}$

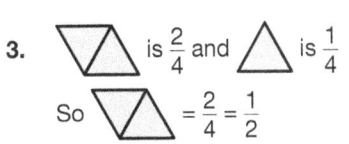

3. ▽▽ is $\frac{2}{4}$ and △ is $\frac{1}{4}$
   So ▽▽ = $\frac{2}{4}$ = $\frac{1}{2}$

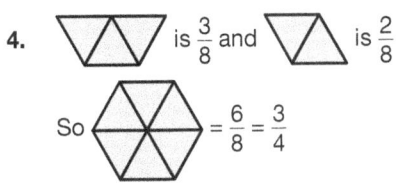

4. ▽▽▽ is $\frac{3}{8}$ and ▽▽ is $\frac{2}{8}$
   So ⬡ = $\frac{6}{8}$ = $\frac{3}{4}$

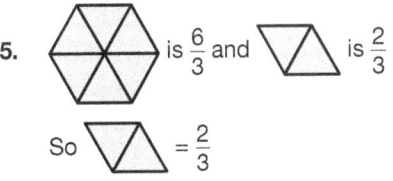

5. ⬡ is $\frac{6}{3}$ and ▽▽ is $\frac{2}{3}$
   So ▽▽ = $\frac{2}{3}$

APM 361
Rounding up or rounding down?

1. Round down to 34 spiders
2. Round up to 16 boxes
3. Round down to 4 tickets
4. Round down to 8 boxes
5. Round down to 46 coats
6. Round up to 3 coaches
7. Round down to 5 balloons

APM 363
Spirals

$0 < 0{\cdot}000001 < \frac{1}{15} < 10\% = \frac{1}{10} < \frac{2}{10} = \frac{1}{5} <$
$22\% < \frac{1}{4} < 0{\cdot}34567 < \frac{3}{8} < 38\% < 0{\cdot}5 < \frac{5}{9} <$
$0{\cdot}56 < 61\% < 68\% < 0{\cdot}7 < 0{\cdot}8 < 95\% <$
$0{\cdot}999999 < 1$

APM 364
Magic square

Children should find that they are always adding four numbers that are each in a different row and column, and that the total is always 10.

The eight numbers that are used to make the square add to 10 and you are always adding these same eight numbers in combination so the total will always be 10.

APM 365
Number pyramids

1.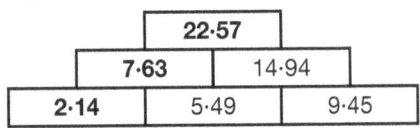

2.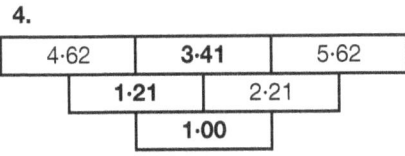

3.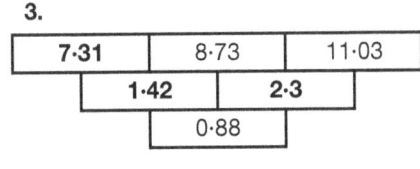

4.
4·62	3·41	5·62
	1·21	2·21
		1·00

APM 366
Freddie says

1. 10% off £25 = £25 − £2·50 = £22·50.
   5% off £22·50 = £22·50 − £1·125 = £21·375
   5% off £25 = £25 − £1·25 = £23·75
   10% off £23·75 = £23·75 − £2·375 = £21·375
   15% off £25 = £25 − 3·75 = £21.25
   It does make a difference and Freddie should take 15% off straight away because then he will save the most money.

2. 10% off £50 = £50 − £5 = £45   10% off £100 = £100 − £10 = £90
   5% off £45 = £45 − £2·25 = £42·75   5% off £90 = £90 − £4·50 = £85·50
   5% off £50 = £50 − £2·50 = £47·50   5% off £100 = £100 − £5 = £95
   10% off £47·50 = £47·50 − 4·75 = £42·75   10% off £95 = £95 − £9·50 = 85·50
   15% off £50 = £50 − £7·50 = £42·50   15% off £100 = £100 − £15 = £85
   The most money is still saved when taking the 15% straight off the price.

3. 10% off £40 = £40 − 4 = 36
   5% added on to £36 = £36 + £1·80 = £37·80
   5% added on to £40 = £40 + £2 = £42
   10% off £42 = £42 − £4·20 = £37·80
   The 5% VAT can be added on before or after the sale and the price will still be the same.

APM 367
What's the percentage?

1. a) 50%   b) 25%   c) 60%   d) 75%
2. a) 50%   b) 75%   c) 40%   d) 25%
3. a) 12 shaded, 12 unshaded   b) 6 shaded, 18 unshaded
   c) 12 shaded, 8 unshaded   d) 12 shaded, 4 unshaded
4. a) 50% shaded, 50% unshaded   b) 25% shaded, 75% unshaded
   c) 60% shaded, 40% unshaded   d) 75% shaded, 25% unshaded
5. 6 shaded, 34 unshaded
6. 14 shaded, 26 unshaded
7. 10 shaded, 30 unshaded
8. 12·8 shaded, 27·2 unshaded

Drawings will vary.

Algebraic Thinking Pupil Book 3

Page 3
Number sequences

1. 125, 150, 175, 200
2. 975, 1000, 1025, 1050
3. 100, 75, 50, 25
4. 700, 725, 750, 775
5. 88, 113, 138, 163
6. 199, 224, 249, 274
7. 181, 156, 131, 106
8. 102, 127, 152, 177
9. Difference is 4
   36, 40, 44
10. Difference is 3
    19, 22, 25
11. Difference is 5
    36, 41, 46
12. Difference is 6
    72, 78, 84
13. Difference is 5
    37, 42, 47
14. Difference is 6
    3, -3, -9
15. Difference is 3
    3, 0, -3
16. Difference is 3
    1, -2, -5

Rocket 13 steps to get over 100; 26 steps to get over 200.

Page 4
Exploring number sequences

1. 90, 115, 140, 165, 190
2. 60, 75, 90, 105, 120
3. 44, 55, 66, 77, 88
4. 108, 96, 84, 72, 60
5. 64, 80, 96, 112, 128
6. 29, 36, 43, 50, 57
7. 20, 14, 8, 2, -4
8. 32, 37, 42, 47, 52
9. Difference is 15
   2, 17, 32, ...
10. Difference is 5
    2, 7, 12, 17, ...
11. Difference is 6
    4, 10, 16, 22, ...
12. Difference is 6
    1, 7, 13, 19, ...
13. Difference is 4
    3, 7, 11, 15, 19, 23, ...
14. Difference is 5
    3, 8, 13, 18, 23, 28, 33, 38, ...
15. Difference is 3
    2, 5, 8, 11, 14, 17, 20, 23, 26, 29, ...
16. Difference is 3
    1, 4, 7, 10, 13, 16, 19, 22, 25, 28, 31, ...

Rocket Counting on in 17s from 0. Answers will vary.

Page 5
Fraction sequences

1. 4, $4\frac{1}{2}$, 5, $5\frac{1}{2}$
2. $\frac{8}{10}$, $\frac{9}{10}$, 1, $1\frac{1}{10}$
3. $1\frac{9}{10}$, $2\frac{1}{10}$, $2\frac{3}{10}$, $2\frac{5}{10}$
4. $2\frac{1}{2}$, $2\frac{3}{4}$, 3, $3\frac{1}{4}$
5. 6, $6\frac{1}{2}$, 7, $7\frac{1}{2}$
6. 9, $10\frac{1}{2}$, 12, $13\frac{1}{2}$
7. 6, $4\frac{1}{2}$, 3, $1\frac{1}{2}$
8. $1\frac{2}{3}$, 2, $2\frac{1}{3}$, $2\frac{2}{3}$
9. 8, $8\frac{3}{4}$, $9\frac{1}{2}$, $10\frac{1}{4}$
10. 20, $22\frac{1}{2}$, 25, $27\frac{1}{2}$
11. $3\frac{1}{3}$, 4
12. $3\frac{3}{4}$, $4\frac{1}{4}$
13. $4\frac{1}{3}$, 5
14. $2\frac{1}{4}$, $3\frac{3}{4}$, $5\frac{1}{4}$

Rocket Answers will vary.

Page 6
Number patterns

1. 26, 32, 38, 44, 50, 56, 62, 68, 74
2. 6, 13, 20, 27, 34, 41, 48, 55, 62
   23, 29, 35, 41, 47, 53, 59, 65, 71
   3·4, 3·9, 4·4, 4·9, 5·4, 5·9, 6·4, 6·9, 7·4
   1·9, 2·2, 2·5, 2·8, 3·1, 3·4, 3·7, 4, 4·3
   $7\frac{1}{4}$, $7\frac{1}{2}$, $7\frac{3}{4}$, 8, $8\frac{1}{4}$, $8\frac{1}{2}$, $8\frac{3}{4}$, 9, $9\frac{1}{4}$
   $4\frac{3}{5}$, $4\frac{4}{5}$, 5, $5\frac{1}{5}$, $5\frac{2}{5}$, $5\frac{3}{5}$, $5\frac{4}{5}$, 6, $6\frac{1}{5}$

Rocket

90	91	92	93	94	95	96	97	98	99
80	81	82	83	84	85	86	87	88	89
70	71	72	73	74	75	76	77	78	79
60	61	62	63	64	65	66	67	68	69
50	51	52	53	54	55	56	57	58	59
40	41	42	43	44	45	46	47	48	49
30	31	32	33	34	35	36	37	38	39
20	21	22	23	24	25	26	27	28	29
10	11	12	13	14	15	16	17	18	19
0	1	2	3	4	5	6	7	8	9

The pattern alternates between the two colours vertically. Also all odd numbers and even numbers under 4 are left white.

Page 7
Number sequences

1. 67; 45, 34, 23, 12, 1
2. 4; $3\frac{1}{3}$, 3, $2\frac{2}{3}$, $2\frac{1}{3}$, 2
3. $5\frac{3}{4}$, 6, $6\frac{1}{4}$; $6\frac{3}{4}$; $7\frac{1}{4}$, $7\frac{1}{2}$, $7\frac{3}{4}$, 8, $8\frac{1}{4}$
4. 3·4, 3·5; 3·7, 3·8, 3·9, 4·0, 4·1
5. $2\frac{1}{2}$, 4; $5\frac{1}{2}$, $6\frac{1}{4}$, 7, $7\frac{3}{4}$, $8\frac{1}{2}$
6. 5·4, 6·6; 9, 10·2, 11·4, 12·6, 13·8
7. 5, $5\frac{1}{3}$; 6, $6\frac{1}{3}$, $6\frac{2}{3}$, 7, $7\frac{1}{3}$
8. 3·06, 3·07; 3·09, 3·10 (or 3·1), 3·11, 3·12, 3·13

Rocket Answers will vary.

9–12. Answers will vary.

Page 8
Number patterns

1. 95, 191, 383; difference doubles each time
2. 22, 29, 37; difference increases by 1 each time
3. 16, 32, 64, 128; double the previous number
4. 52, 66, 82; difference increases by 2 each time
5. 25, 36, 49, 64; multiply successive numbers by themselves (to get square numbers)
6. 40, 30, 19; subtract a number which increases by 1 each time and starts at 5
7. 320, 640, 1280, 2560; double the previous number
8. 65, 83, 104; add on successive multiples of 3 each time
9. Answers will vary.

Rocket

90	91	92	93	94	95	96	97	98	99
80	81	82	83	84	85	86	87	88	89
70	71	72	73	74	75	76	77	78	79
60	61	62	63	64	65	66	67	68	69
50	51	52	53	54	55	56	57	58	59
40	41	42	43	44	45	46	47	48	49
30	31	32	33	34	35	36	37	38	39
20	21	22	23	24	25	26	27	28	29
10	11	12	13	14	15	16	17	18	19
0	1	2	3	4	5	6	7	8	9

The sequence increases by 12 each time. Children's description of the pattern will vary, but should note its regularity.

Page 9
Function machines

1.

In	425	200	382	430	675	898
Out	775	550	732	780	1025	1248

2.

In	650	800	518	1111	1386	701
Out	225	375	93	686	961	276

3. × 3
4. ÷ 9
5. − 125
6. + 345

Rocket Answers will vary.

7.

In	Function	Out
16	halve	8
260	halve	130
150	halve	75
326	halve	163

In	Function	Out
32	quarter	8
80	quarter	20
500	quarter	125
344	quarter	86

Page 10
Function machines

1.
In	Out
3	15
6	30
8	40
9	45
12	60

2.
In	Out
4	32
6	48
8	64
14	112
22	176

3.
In	Out
3	18
12	72
7	42
5	30
24	144

4.
In	Out
4	28
16	112
10	70
26	182
6	42

Rocket Answers will vary.

5.
In	40	70	6	80	900
Out	400	700	60	800	9000

6.
In	5	7	6	8	20
Out	45	63	54	72	180

Page 11
Equal (=) or not equal (≠)?

1. $23 + 18 \neq 26 + 17$
2. $186 - 45 \neq 174 - 31$
3. $64 + 19 = 39 + 44$
4. $351 - 135 = 374 - 158$
5. $73 + 52 \neq 94 + 21$
6. $408 - 75 \neq 524 - 123$
7. $18 + 35 = 36 + 27$
8. $724 - 57 = 686 - 19$
9. $14 + 52 = 98 - 32$
10. $625 - 586 = 68 - 29$
11. $363 + 146 = 258 + 251$
12. $433 - 391 = 167 - 128$

Rocket Answers will vary.

Page 12
Balancing equations

1. $5 \times 8 = 4 \times 10$
2. $10 \times 2 = 4 \times 5$
3. $7 \times 6 = 3 \times 14$
4. $6 \times 4 = 3 \times 8$
5. $5 \times 8 = 2 \times 20$
6. $5 \times 12 = 10 \times 6$
7. $63 \div 7 = 45 \div 5$
8. $72 \div 8 \neq 36 \div 6$
9. $64 \div 8 \neq 42 \div 6$
10. $56 \div 7 = 24 \div 3$
11. $240 \div 3 = 160 \div 2$
12. $350 \div 7 = 400 \div 8$
13. $48 \div 4 \neq 5 \times 3$
14. $120 \div 10 = 6 \times 2$

Rocket The first number on the left-hand side of the equation has been doubled, and the second halved, to produce the numbers on the right-hand side. Answers will vary.

Page 13
Greater than, less than

1. $350 > 30 \times 9$
2. $12 > 49 \div 7$
3. $40 \times 3 < 140$
4. $36 < \frac{1}{2}$ of 80
5. $600 \div 3 > 2$
6. $67 > 295 \div 5$
7. $565 \div 5 > 103$
8. $43 \times 3 > 119$
9. Answers must be greater than 126.
10. Answers must be less than 105.
11. Answers must be less than 43.
12. Answers must be less than 360.
13. Answers must be less than 6.
14. Answers must be less than 62.
15. Answers must be less than 8
16. Answers must be greater than 4·2.
17. Answers must be less than 6.
18. Answers must be less than 5.

Rocket Answers will vary.

Page 14
Number pairs

1. 1 + 4
   2 + 3
   5 + 0
2. 1 + 5
   2 + 4
   3 + 3
   6 + 0
3. 1 + 6
   2 + 5
   3 + 4
   7 + 0
4. 1 + 7
   2 + 6
   3 + 5
   4 + 4
   8 + 0
5. 1 + 8
   2 + 7
   3 + 6
   4 + 5
   9 + 0
6. 1 + 9
   2 + 8
   3 + 7
   4 + 6
   5 + 5
   10 + 0

1. 3
2. 4
3. 4
4. 5
5. 5
6. 6
7. 6
8. 7
9. 7
10. 8
11. 8
12. In this pattern two consecutive numbers have the same amount of number pairs. This happens because two identical numbers are added to make an even number, and two consecutive numbers are added to make the following odd number. For example:
    0 + 6 = 6   1 + 5 = 6
    2 + 4 = 6   3 + 3 = 6
    0 + 7 = 7   1 + 6 = 7
    2 + 5 = 7   3 + 4 = 7
13. The rule for even numbers is:
    $p = (n \div 2) + 1$ where p is the total number of number pairs and n is the number that the number pairs are a total of.
    The rule for odd numbrs is:
    $p = (n \div 2) + 0·5$ where p is the total number of number pairs and n is the number that the number pairs are a total of.

Rocket Answers will vary. Children will find that there is no pattern for number trios.

Page 15
Symbols representing numbers

1. $25 + 500 = 525$
2. $100 + 25 = 125$
3. $75 + 100 + 500 = 675$
4. $25 + 75 + 100 = 200$
5. $100 \times 25 = 2500$
6. $75 \times 100 = 7500$
7. $100 \div 25 = 4$
8. $25 \div 100 = 0·25$
9. $500 + 75 - 100 = 475$
10. $500 + 25 + 75 - 100 = 500$

Rocket Answers will vary.

Page 16
Letters representing numbers

1. $a + b = 5 + 20 = 25$
2. $b + c = 20 + 45 = 65$
3. $d + c = 40 + 45 = 85$
4. $f - a = 10 - 5 = 5$
5. $c \div a = 45 \div 5 = 9$
6. $f \times b = 10 \times 20 = 200$
7. $c \times f = 45 \times 10 = 450$
8. $b \times a = 20 \times 5 = 100$

9. $d \times a = 40 \times 5 = 200$
10. $b \div a = 20 \div 5 = 4$
11. $f \div a = 10 \div 5 = 2$
12. $c \div f = 45 \div 10 = 4 \cdot 5$
13. $e + d + f = 8 + 40 + 10 = 58$
14. $e + c + e = 8 + 45 + 8 = 61$
15. $a \times f \times b = 5 \times 10 \times 20 = 1000$
16. $e \times f \times f = 8 \times 10 \times 10 = 800$
17. Answers will vary.

Rocket Answers will vary.

Page 17
Solving simple equations

1. $n = 11$
2. $n = 17$
3. $n = 17$
4. $n = 26$
5. $n = 16$
6. $n = 16$
7. $n = 25$
8. $n = 16$
9. $n = 26$
10. $n = 25$
11. $n = 35$
12. $n = 75$
13. $n = 11$
14. $n = 4$
15. $n = 32$
16. $n = 30$
17. $n = 8$
18. $n = 8$

Rocket $e = 5$.
Answers will vary.

Page 18
Growing patterns

Children's answers may differ from those given and yet be valid. Ask for an explanation.

1. Each arm of the cross increases by one cube each time; the total number of cubes increases by 4 each time.
2. Each arm of the L-shape grows by two lines each time; the total number of lines increases by 4 each time.
3. Each row of red cubes increases by two cubes each time and the column of grey cubes increases by one each time; the total number of cubes increases by 5 each time.

Rocket Answers will vary.

Page 19
Square numbers

1.
2.
3.
4.
5.
6.
7. $4^2 = 16$
8. $7^2 = 49$
9. $2^2 = 4$
10. $9^2 = 81$
11. $6^2 = 36$
12. $8^2 = 64$
13. $5^2 = 25$
14. $1^2 = 1$
15. $3^2 = 9$
16. $10^2 = 100$
17. $0^2 = 0$
18. $11^2 = 121$

Rocket Answers may vary, but 25, 36, 49 and 81 use a maximum of eight cards.

Page 20
Square numbers

1. $7^2 = 49$
2. $2^2 = 4$
3. $10^2 = 100$
4. $3^2 = 9$
5. $8^2 = 64$
6. $1^2 = 1$
7. $9^2 = 81$
8. $5^2 = 25$
9. $6^2 = 36$

10.

10^2	20^2	30^2	40^2	50^2	60^2	70^2	80^2	90^2	100^2
100	400	900	1600	2500	3600	4900	6400	8100	10 000

Rocket The happy numbers up to, and including 100 are: 1, 7, 10, 13, 19, 23, 28, 31, 32, 44, 49, 68, 70, 79, 82, 86, 91, 94, 97, 100.

Page 21
Notation for square and cube numbers

1. $3^2 = 3 \times 3 = 9$
2. $5^2 = 5 \times 5 = 25$
3. $4^2 = 4 \times 4 = 16$
4. $6^2 = 6 \times 6 = 36$
5. $3^3 = 3 \times 3 \times 3 = 27$
6. $5^3 = 5 \times 5 \times 5 = 125$
7. $4^3 = 4 \times 4 \times 4 = 64$
8. $6^3 = 6 \times 6 \times 6 = 216$
9. $2^3 = 2 \times 2 \times 2 = 8$
10. $1^3 = 1 \times 1 \times 1 = 1$
11. $10^3 = 10 \times 10 \times 10 = 1000$
12. $9^3 = 9 \times 9 \times 9 = 729$

Rocket
$1^2 = 1, 1^3 = 1$
$2^2 = 4, 2^3 = 8$
$3^2 = 9, 3^3 = 27$
$4^2 = 16, 4^3 = 64$
$5^2 = 25, 5^3 = 125$
$6^2 = 36, 6^3 = 216$
$7^2 = 49, 7^3 = 343$
$8^2 = 64, 8^3 = 512$
$9^2 = 81, 9^3 = 729$
$10^2 = 100, 10^3 = 1000$
$11^2 = 121, 11^3 = 1331$
$12^2 = 144, 12^3 = 1728$
$13^2 = 169, 13^3 = 2197$
$14^2 = 196, 14^3 = 2744$
$15^2 = 225, 15^3 = 3375$
$16^2 = 256, 16^3 = 4096$
$17^2 = 289, 17^3 = 4913$
$18^2 = 324, 18^3 = 5832$
$19^2 = 361, 19^3 = 6859$
$20^2 = 400, 20^3 = 8000$

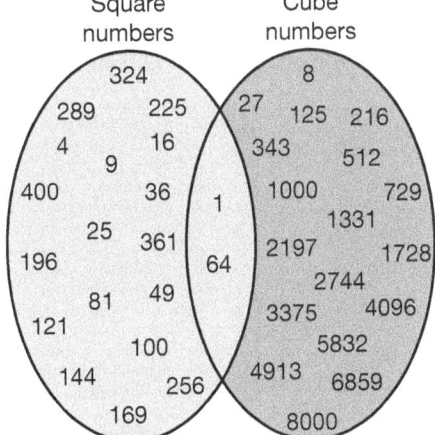

Page 22
Triangular number patterns

1.

Spots pattern	Number of dots in each row	Total of dots	How many were added?
•	1	1	
(2-row pattern)	1, 2	3	2
(3-row pattern)	1, 2, 3	6	3
(4-row pattern)	1, 2, 3, 4	10	4
(5-row pattern)	1, 2, 3, 4, 5	15	5

Answers will vary.

Rocket John plans to pile the boxes up in a triangle with six rows, and six boxes on the bottom row. Six rows of 10 cm boxes will need 60 cm height clearance.

Page 23
Triangular number patterns

1. 1 match
2. 3 matches
3. 6 matches
4. 10 matches
5. These are triangular numbers.
6. 45 matches
7. 66 matches
8. 300 matches
9. 861 matches
10. 4950 matches

Rocket Answers will vary.

Page 24
Triangular number patterns

1. 6 paths
2. 10 paths
3. 15 paths
4. 21 paths
5. These are triangular numbers.
6. 45 paths
7. 120 paths
8. 1485 paths

Rocket The pattern is that the number of journeys is double the number of paths and therefore double the triangular number. The rule for working out the number of journeys is $j = n(n - 1)$ where j is the total number of journeys and n is the total number of attractions. The rule for working out the number of paths for any number of attractions is therefore $p = \dfrac{n(n - 1)}{2}$ where p is the total number of paths and n is the total number of attractions.

Page 25
Cube number patterns

1. 1 flat
2. 8 flats
3. 27 flats
4. 64 flats
5. 125 flats
6. 216 flats
7. These are cube numbers.
8. If you cube the number of flats high that the building is you will find how many flats are in a building. You can show this by saying $f = n^3$ where f is the total number of flats and n is how many flats high the tower block is.
9. 5 squares of paint
10. 20 squares of paint
11. 45 squares of paint
12. 80 squares of paint
13. 125 squares of paint
14. 180 squares of paint
15. These are square numbers multiplied by 5.
16. You must square the number of flats there are to find the number of squares to be painted on one side of the building and then multiply it by 5 to find the total number of squares. The rule is $s = 5(n^2)$ where s is the number of squares of paint and n is the number of flats.

Rocket Answers will vary.

Page 26
Pascal's triangle

1. The coloured numbers are all triangular numbers.
2. Answers will vary.
3. 1
   1 + 1 = 2
   1 + 2 + 1 = 4
   1 + 3 + 3 + 1 = 8
   1 + 4 + 6 + 4 + 1 = 16
   1 + 5 + 10 + 10 + 5 + 1 = 32
   1 + 6 + 15 + 20 + 15 + 6 + 1 = 64
   1 + 7 + 21 + 35 + 35 + 21 + 7 + 1 = 128
   1 + 8 + 28 + 56 + 70 + 56 + 28 + 8 + 1 = 256
   1 + 9 + 36 + 84 + 126 + 126 + 84 + 36 + 9 + 1 = 512
   1 + 10 + 45 + 120 + 210 + 252 + 210 + 120 + 45 + 10 + 1 = 1024
   1 + 11 + 55 + 165 + 330 + 462 + 462 + 330 + 165 + 55 + 11 + 1 = 2048
   1 + 12 + 66 + 220 + 495 + 792 + 924 + 792 + 495 + 220 + 66 + 12 + 1 = 4096
   1 + 13 + 78 + 186 + 715 + 1287 + 1716 + 1716 + 1287 + 715 + 186 + 78 + 13 + 1 = 7992

Page 27
Fibonacci's pattern

1. Add two adjacent numbers to make the next number in the sequence.
2. 1, 1, 2, 3, 5, 8, 13, 21, 34, 55, 89, 144, ...
3. Answers will vary.
4. 5, 6, 11, 17
5. 2, 10, 12, 22
6. 8, 11, 19, 30
7. 1, 10, 11, 21
8. 7, 15, 22, 37, 59
9. 7, 16, 23, 39, 62
10. 8, 28, 36, 64, 100

Rocket

	1	1	2	3	5	8	13	21	34	55	89	144
Multiple of 2			x			x			x			x
Multiple of 3				x				x				x
Multiple of 4						x						x
Multiple of 5					x					x		

In the first twelve numbers, multiples of 2 appear every three numbers; multiples of 3 appear every four numbers; multiples of 4 appear every six numbers; multiples of 5 appear every five numbers.

Page 28
Two-step function machines

1.
In	Out
2	8
5	17
7	23
10	32
4	14
8	26
3	11

2.
In	Out
5	17
3	9
6	21
9	33
1	1
4	13
7	25

3.
In	Out
6	14
4	8
8	20
10	26
11	29
5	11
7	17

4.
In	Out
3	19
5	29
7	39
10	54
8	44
11	59
4	24

Rocket
1. Output − 2 ÷ 3 → input
2. Output + 3 ÷ 4 → input
3. Output + 4 ÷ 3 → input
4. Output − 4 ÷ 5 → input

Page 29
Two-step function machines

1.

In	Step 1: × 10	Step 2: + 7
15	150	157
27	270	277
38	380	387

2.

In	Step 1: × 9	Step 2: − 6
20	180	174
35	315	309
76	684	678

3.

In	Step 1: ÷ 10	Step 2: + 25
360	36	61
570	57	82
2050	205	230

4.

In	Step 1: ÷ 100	Step 2: − 39
48 000	480	441
7500	75	36
6300	63	24

Rocket

	In	Step 1: reverse digits	Step 2 and out: subtract
Machine A	863	368	495

	In	Step 1: reverse digits	Step 2 and out: add
Machine B	495	594	1089

	In	Step 1: reverse digits	Step 2 and out: subtract
Machine A	794	497	297

	In	Step 1: reverse digits	Step 2 and out: add
Machine B	297	792	1089

Answers will vary, but the answers are all divisible by 11.

Page 30
Two-step function machines

1.

In	Out red	Out blue
8	44	41
14	80	77
32	188	185
50	296	293
11	62	59
17	98	95
22	128	125

2.

In	Out red	Out blue
49	52	132
119	122	342
376	379	1113
268	271	789
501	504	1488
99	102	282
80	83	225

3. 10   **4.** 12
5. 5   **6.** 100
7. 10   **8.** 12
9. 5   **10.** 39

Page 31
Creating expressions

The letters and expressions that children use for questions **1-15** may vary but the numbers should not.

1. $6c$
2. $5h$
3. $4t$
4. $7w$
5. $4m$
6. $5g$
7. $5a$
8. $3o$
9. $7b$
10. $8b + 4o$
11. $6a + 2k$
12. $2m + 5o$
13. $3b + 2a + 4k$
14. $4o + 7k + 3b$
15. $3k + 4a + 2m$

Rocket Answers may vary.

Page 32
Expressions from number grids

1.

31	32	33
$n+9$	$n+10$	$n+11$
21	22	23
$n-1$	n	$n+1$
11	12	13
$n-11$	$n-10$	$n-9$

2.

63	64	65
$n+9$	$n+10$	$n+11$
53	54	55
$n-1$	n	$n+1$
43	44	45
$n-11$	$n-10$	$n-9$

Rocket Grid 1: $n + 9 + n + 10 + n + 11 + n - 1 + n + n + 1 + n - 11 + n - 10 + n - 9 = 9n$
$31 + 32 + 33 + 21 + 22 + 23 + 11 + 12 + 13 = 198$
$198 = 9n$
$198 ÷ 9 = n$
$22 = n$

Grid 2: $n + 9 + n + 10 + n + 11 + n - 1 + n + n + 1 + n - 11 + n - 10 + n - 9 = 9n$
$63 + 64 + 65 + 53 + 54 + 55 + 43 + 44 + 45 = 486$
$486 = 9n$
$486 ÷ 9 = n$
$54 = n$

This does always work.
Answers will vary.

Page 33
Triangular and square numbers

1.

Position	Triangular number	Made by adding
1st	1	1
2nd	3	1 + 2
3rd	6	1 + 2 + 3
4th	10	1 + 2 + 3 + 4
5th	15	1 + 2 + 3 + 4 + 5
6th	21	1 + 2 + 3 + 4 + 5 + 6
7th	28	1 + 2 + 3 + 4 + 5 + 6 + 7
8th	36	1 + 2 + 3 + 4 + 5 + 6 + 7 + 8
9th	45	1 + 2 + 3 + 4 + 5 + 6 + 7 + 8 + 9
10th	55	1 + 2 + 3 + 4 + 5 + 6 + 7 + 8 + 9 + 10

2.

Position	Square number	Made by multiplying	Made by adding triangular numbers	Position of triangular numbers
1st	1	1 × 1	1	1st
2nd	4	2 × 2	1 + 3	1st and 2nd
3rd	9	3 × 3	3 + 6	2nd and 3rd
4th	16	4 × 4	6 + 10	3rd and 4th
5th	25	5 × 5	10 + 15	4th and 5th
6th	36	6 × 6	15 + 21	5th and 6th
7th	49	7 × 7	21 + 28	6th and 7th
8th	64	8 × 8	28 + 36	7th and 8th
9th	81	9 × 9	36 + 45	8th and 9th
10th	100	10 × 10	45 + 55	9th and 10th

3. $n \times n$, or n^2
4. Yes this applies beyond the 10th term. The pattern of triangular numbers is made by adding on 1, 2, 3,... and so on. Start with 55, which is odd: adding on an odd number (11) produces an even number (O+O=E). Next, add on an even number (12) and you still get an even number (E+E=E). The next number to be added on (13) is odd, giving an odd total (E+O=O). And so the pattern continues.

Rocket Answers will vary.

Page 34
Matchstick patterns

1. Sequence B: 7 matchsticks for the first pattern, 12 matchsticks for the second pattern, 17 matchsticks for the third pattern
   Sequence C: 10 matchsticks for the first pattern, 17 matchsticks for the second pattern, 24 matchsticks for the third pattern

2.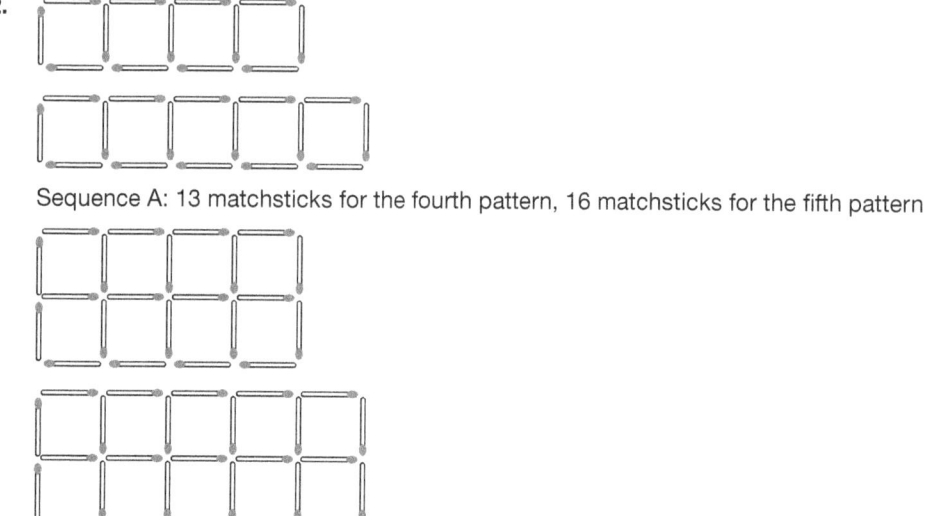

Sequence A: 13 matchsticks for the fourth pattern, 16 matchsticks for the fifth pattern

Sequence B: 22 matchsticks for the fourth pattern, 27 matchsticks for the fifth pattern

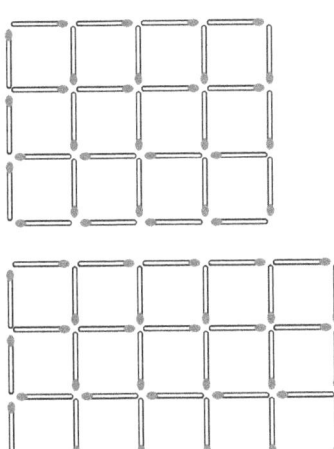

Sequence C: 31 matchsticks for the fourth pattern, 38 matchsticks for the fifth pattern

3.

	1st pattern	2nd pattern	3rd pattern	4th pattern	5th pattern
Sequence A	4	7	10	13	16
Sequence B	7	12	17	22	27
Sequence C	10	17	24	31	38

4. Sequence A: 10th pattern, 31 matchsticks
Sequence B: 10th pattern, 52 matchsticks
Sequence C: 10th pattern, 73 matchsticks

Rocket Sequence A: Pattern number × 3 + 1 or $3n + 1$
Sequence B: Pattern number × 5 + 2 or $5n + 2$
Sequence C: Pattern number × 7 + 3 or $7n + 3$

Page 35

Straw patterns

1. 3 straws
2. 1 triangle
3. 9 straws
4. 4 small triangles
5. 18 straws
6. 9 small triangles

7.

Shape	1	2	3	4	5	6	7	8	9	10
Triangular number	1	3	6	10	15	21	28	36	45	55
Number of small triangles	1	4	9	16	25	36	49	64	81	100
Number of straws	3	9	18	30	45	63	84	108	135	165

8. Answers will vary.
9. Shape 12: 144 small triangles (i.e. 12 × 12, as the sequence matches the sequence of square numbers)
Shape 15: 225 small triangles (i.e. 15 × 15)
Shape 20: 400 small triangles (i.e. 20 × 20)
Shape 100: 10 000 small triangles (i.e. 100 × 100)
10. Number of straws: nth term = number of small triangles + triangular number + n
Number of small triangles: nth term = n^2

Rocket

Shape	1	2	3	10	20	100	n
Number of small diamonds	1	4	9	100	400	10 000	n^2
Number of straws	4	12	24	220	840	20 200	$2n^2 + 2n$

Page 36

Rules of pattern

1.
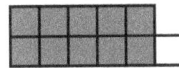 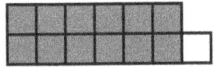

2. Answers will vary.

3.

Position	Number of squares
1	3
2	5
3	7
4	9
5	11
6	13

4. Answers will vary.

5. The number of squares increases by 2 each time. If you multiply its position by 2 and then add 1 you find the number of squares.
6. 81, 201
7. The rule for the function machine would be: × 2 + 1.

Rocket The numbers in the right-hand column would increase by 1. The new function would be: × 2 + 2.

Page 37
Rules of pattern

1.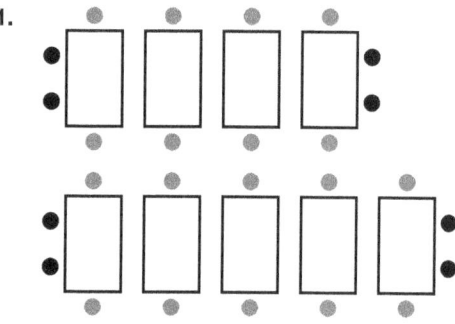

2.
Number of tables	1	2	3	4	5	6
Number of chairs	6	8	10	12	14	16

3.
Number of tables	1	2	3	4	5	6	10	40
Number of chairs	6	8	10	12	14	16	24	44

4. There are always twice as many red chairs as tables.

Rocket The number of red chairs would stay the same. There would be twice as many blue chairs each time — four times the number of tables.

Page 38
Drawing an expression

1. Children's sketches should show a two-step function machine with × 3 and + 1.
2. Children's sketches should show a two-step function machine with × 2 and + 3.
3. Children's sketches should show a two-step function machine with × 4 and + 5.
4. Children's sketches should show a two-step function machine with × 6 and − 2.
5. Children's sketches should show a two-step function machine with × 4 and − 3.
6. Children's sketches should show a two-step function machine with × 6 and − 4.
7. Children's sketches should show a two-step function machine with × 8 and − 2.
8. Children's sketches should show a two-step function machine with × 3 and + 7.
9. Children's sketches should show a two-step function machine with × 4 and − 2.
10. Function machine 5
11. Function machine 9
12. Function machine 8
13. Function machine 3

Rocket Answers will vary.

Page 39
Inverse functions

1. ÷ 5
2. ÷ 7
3. × 4
4. × 3
5. − 6
6. + 4
7. + 325
8. − 735
9. + 0·9
10. × 20
11. ÷ 26
12. × 45
13. $n - 3$
14. $n - 8$
15. $n - 6$
16. $n - 3$
17. $n + 2$
18. $n + 5$
19. $n + 4$
20. $n + 6$
21. $\frac{n}{5}$ (or $n ÷ 5$)
22. $\frac{n}{3}$ (or $n ÷ 3$)
23. $\frac{n}{6}$ (or $n ÷ 6$)
24. $\frac{n}{18}$ (or $n ÷ 18$)
25. $\frac{n}{4}$ (or $n ÷ 4$)
26. $\frac{n}{8}$ (or $n ÷ 8$)
27. $7n$
28. $10n$
29.
In	Out
4	8
8	16
12	24

30.
In	Out
5	7
7	9
10	12

In	Out
5	2·5
7	3·5
10	5

The inverse of $2n$ is $\frac{n}{2}$.

The inverse of $n + 2$ is $n - 2$.

The inverse of $\frac{1}{2}n$ is $\frac{n}{2}$ (or $n ÷ 2$).

Rocket Answers will vary.

Page 40
Solving equations

1. Children's drawings should show a two-step function machine showing that: $x × 3 = 3x$ and then $3x + 4 = 16$.
They should then show the inverse of this function machine to find the solution: $16 - 4 = 12$ and then $12 ÷ 3 = 4$ and therefore $x = 4$.

2. Children's drawings should show a two-step function machine showing that: $n × 2 = 2n$ and then $2n - 4 = 2$.
They should then show the inverse of this function machine to find the solution: $2 + 4 = 6$ and then $6 ÷ 2 = 3$ and therefore $n = 3$.

3. Children's drawings should show a two-step function machine showing that: $n × \frac{1}{2} = \frac{1}{2}n$ and then $\frac{1}{2}n + 7 = 13$.
They should then show the inverse of this function machine to find the solution: $13 - 7 = 6$ and then $6 × 2 = 12$ and therefore $n = 12$.

4. Children's drawings should show a two-step function machine showing that: $s × \frac{1}{2} = \frac{1}{2}s$ and then $\frac{1}{2}s - 5 = 5$.
They should then show the inverse of this function machine to find the solution: $5 + 5 = 10$ and then $10 × 2 = 20$ and therefore $s = 20$.

5. Children's drawings should show a two-step function machine showing that: $p × 7 = 7p$ and then $7p + 2 = 142$.
They should then show the inverse of this function machine to find the solution: $142 - 2 = 140$ and then $140 ÷ 7 = 20$ and therefore $p = 20$.

6. Children's drawings should show a two-step function machine showing that: $q × 3 = 3q$ and then $3q - 10 = 20$.
They should then show the inverse of this function machine to find the solution: $20 + 10 = 30$ and then $30 ÷ 3 = 10$ and therefore $q = 10$.

7. Children's drawings should show a two-step function machine showing that: $t × \frac{1}{4} = \frac{1}{4}t$ and then $\frac{1}{4}t + 3 = 8$.
They should then show the inverse of this function machine to find the solution: $8 - 3 = 5$ and then $5 × 4 = 20$ and therefore $t = 20$.

8. Children's drawings should show a two-step function machine showing that: $m × \frac{1}{10} = \frac{1}{10}m$ and then $\frac{1}{10}m - 15 = 9$.

They should then show the inverse of this function machine to find the solution: 9 + 15 = 24 and then 24 × 10 = 240 and therefore $m = 240$.

9. Children's drawings should show a two-step function machine showing that: $x \times \frac{1}{5} = \frac{1}{5}x$ and then $\frac{1}{5}x - 7 = 10$.
They should then show the inverse of this function machine to find the solution: 10 + 7 = 17 and then 17 × 5 = 85 and therefore $x = 85$.

10. Children's drawings should show a two-step function machine showing that: $p \times \frac{1}{4} = \frac{1}{4}p$ and then $\frac{1}{4}p + 9 = 13$.
They should then show the inverse of this function machine to find the solution: 13 − 9 = 4 and then 4 × 4 = 16 and therefore $p = 16$.

Rocket Answers will vary.

Page 41
Solving equations

1. Children's drawings should show a two-step function machine showing that: $x + 4 = (x + 4)$ and then $(x + 4) \times 3 = 18$.
They should then show the inverse of this function machine to find the solution: 18 ÷ 3 = 6 and then 6 − 4 = 2 and therefore $x = 2$.

2. Children's drawings should show a two-step function machine showing that: $y + 5 = (y + 5)$ and then $(y + 5) \times 2 = 18$.
They should then show the inverse of this function machine to find the solution: 18 ÷ 2 = 9 and then 9 − 5 = 4 and therefore $y = 4$.

3. Children's drawings should show a two-step function machine showing that: $s + 2 = (s + 2)$ and then $(s + 2) \times 3 = 36$.
They should then show the inverse of this function machine to find the solution: 36 ÷ 3 = 12 and then 12 − 2 = 10 and therefore $s = 10$.

4. Children's drawings should show a two-step function machine showing that: $m + 5 = (m + 5)$ and then $(m + 5) \times \frac{1}{2} = 5$.
They should then show the inverse of this function machine to find the solution: 5 × 2 = 10 and then 10 − 5 = 5 and therefore $m = 5$.

5. Children's drawings should show a two-step function machine showing that: $n - 10 = (n - 10)$ and then $(n - 10) \times \frac{1}{2} = 10$.
They should then show the inverse of this function machine to find the solution: 10 × 2 = 20 and then 20 + 10 = 30 and therefore $n = 30$.

6. Children's drawings should show a two-step function machine showing that: $b - \frac{1}{2} = (b - \frac{1}{2})$ and then $(b - \frac{1}{2}) \times 4 = 10$.
They should then show the inverse of this function machine to find the solution: 10 ÷ 4 = 2·5 and then 2·5 + $\frac{1}{2}$ = 3 and therefore $b = 3$.

7. Children's drawings should show a two-step function machine showing that: $d + 2·5 = (d + 2·5)$ and then $(d + 2·5) \times 3 = 12$.
They should then show the inverse of this function machine to find the solution: 12 ÷ 3 = 4 and then 4 − 2·5 = 1·5 and therefore $d = 1·5$.

8. Children's drawings should show a two-step function machine showing that: $f - 3 = (f - 3)$ and then $(f - 3) \times \frac{1}{10} = 1$.
They should then show the inverse of this function machine to find the solution: 1 × 10 = 10 and then 10 + 3 = 13 and therefore $f = 13$.

9. Children's drawings should show a two-step function machine showing that: $p - 4·8 = (p - 4·8)$ and then $(p - 4·8) \times 5 = 17$.
They should then show the inverse of this function machine to find the solution: 17 ÷ 5 = 3·4 and then 3·4 + 4·8 = 8·2 and therefore $p = 8·2$.

10. Children's drawings should show a two-step function machine showing that: $q + 16 = (q + 16)$ and then $(q + 16) \times \frac{1}{4} = 20$.
They should then show the inverse of this function machine to find the solution: 20 × 4 = 80 and then 80 − 16 = 64 and therefore $q = 64$.

Rocket The diagrams that children draw will vary but should demonstrate the following calculations.
$3n = n + 6$
$2n = 6$
$n = 3$
$35 - 2n = 5n$
$35 = 7n$
$n = 5$
$4n = 6 + n$
$3n = 6$
$n = 2$
$3n = 16 + n$
$2n = 16$
$n = 8$

Page 42
Reversing functions

1. Function: $2n - 1$

In n	Step 1 $2n$	Step 2 and out −1
3	6	5
9	18	17
15	30	29
11	22	21
Answers will vary.		
Answers will vary.		

Function: $\frac{1}{n} + 1$

In n	Step 1 $\frac{1}{2}n$	Step 2 and out +1
5	2·5	3·5
17	8·5	9·5
29	14·5	15·5
21	10·5	11·5
Answers will vary.		
Answers will vary.		

2. The tables show that Lorna's assertion is incorrect (and therefore Stuart is correct) because the output of table 2 would be the same as the input of table 1 if Lorna had calculated the inverse of $2n - 1$ correctly.

Rocket Answers will vary.

Page 43
Balancing equations

1. $n = 8$
2. $n = 27$
3. $n = 13$
4. $n = 29$
5. $n = 54$
6. $n = 97$
7. $n = 132$
8. $n = 152$
9. $n = 269$

Rocket The apples weigh 450 g.

Page 44
Balancing equations

1. $n = 9$
2. $n = 28$
3. $n = 44$
4. $n = 65$
5. $n = 111$
6. $n = 142$
7. $n = 262$
8. $n = 264$
9. $n = 335$

Rocket Simon's number is 41. Answers may vary.

Page 45
Balancing equations

1. $n = 9$
2. $n = 8$
3. $n = 15$
4. $n = 7·5$

5. $n = 11$ **6.** $n = 4$
7. $n = 14$ **8.** $n = 12$
9. $n = 13$
Rocket 1 lorry balances 5 cars.

Page 46
Interpreting problems

1. $2n + 3 = 17$
   $2n + 3 - 3 = 17 - 3$
   $2n = 14$
   $n = 7$
2. $3n - 4 = 23$
   $n = 9$
3. $5n + 6 = 26$
   $n = 4$
4. $6n - 8 = 52$
   $n = 10$
5. $8n - 9 = 79$
   $n = 11$

Rocket $3n + 2n - 5 = 15$
   $n = 4$

6. Answers will vary.

Page 47
Interpreting problems

1. Forth:
   $(9 \times 4) + a = 39$
   $36 + a = 39$
   $36 - 36 + a = 39 - 36$
   $a = 3$
   Solway:
   $b = (7 \times 4) + (4 \times 2) - 1$
   $b = 35$

   Dee:
   $(5 \times 4) + (2 \times c) - 4 = 32$
   $c = 8$
   Clyde:
   $(4 \times 4) + (2 \times d) - 9 = 17$
   $d = 5$
   Ness:
   $(4 \times e) + (2 \times 6) = 28$
   $e = 4$
   Tweed:
   $(4 \times 5) + (2 \times f) - 3 = 31$
   $f = 7$
   Tay:
   $(4 \times g) + (2 \times 5) - 2 = 48$
   $g = 10$
   Spey:
   $(4 \times 6) + (2 \times h) - 6 = 36$
   $h = 9$

Rocket Answers will vary.

Algebraic Thinking PPMs

PPM 119
Stepping stones

1-4. Answers will vary.

PPM 120
Number patterns

1.

2	4	6	<u>8</u>	<u>10</u>	12	<u>14</u>	<u>16</u>	<u>18</u>
5	10	15	<u>20</u>	<u>25</u>	<u>30</u>	<u>35</u>	<u>40</u>	<u>45</u>
10	20	30	<u>40</u>	<u>50</u>	<u>60</u>	<u>70</u>	<u>80</u>	<u>90</u>
<u>6</u>	<u>9</u>	12	<u>15</u>	<u>18</u>	<u>21</u>	24	27	<u>30</u>
<u>6</u>	12	<u>18</u>	24	30	<u>36</u>	<u>42</u>	<u>48</u>	<u>54</u>
<u>9</u>	<u>18</u>	27	36	<u>45</u>	<u>54</u>	63	<u>72</u>	<u>81</u>
<u>0</u>	12	<u>24</u>	<u>36</u>	<u>48</u>	60	72	84	<u>96</u>
<u>7</u>	<u>14</u>	<u>21</u>	28	35	42	<u>49</u>	<u>56</u>	<u>63</u>
<u>70</u>	140	<u>210</u>	<u>280</u>	350	420	<u>490</u>	<u>560</u>	<u>630</u>
<u>80</u>	<u>160</u>	240	320	400	<u>480</u>	<u>560</u>	640	<u>720</u>

2. Answers will vary.

PPM 121
Sequences

1. 400, 425, 450, 475
2. 70, 65, 60, 55
3. 57, 52, 47, 42
4. 80, 95, 110, 125
5. 66, 77, 88, 99
6. 43, 50, 57, 64
7. 44, 38, 32, 26
8. 12, $13\frac{1}{2}$, 15, $16\frac{1}{2}$
9. $7\frac{1}{4}$, 7, $6\frac{3}{4}$, $6\frac{1}{2}$
10. $10\frac{2}{3}$, $11\frac{1}{3}$, 12, $12\frac{2}{3}$
11. $10\frac{9}{10}$, $10\frac{5}{10}$, $10\frac{1}{10}$, $9\frac{7}{10}$
12. Answers will vary.

PPM 122
What's the rule?

1. 22; + 6; the rule is 'keep adding one more than last time'.
2. 26, 33; + 3, + 4, + 5, + 6, + 7; the rule is 'keep adding one more than last time'.
3. 25, 20; − 7, − 6, − 5; the rule is 'keep subtracting one less than last time'.
4. 85, 75; − 14, − 13, − 12, − 11, − 10; the rule is 'keep subtracting by one less than the subtraction before'.
5. Answers will vary.

PPM 123
Function machines

1.

Out
3860
1480
2540
5040

2.

Out
3720
1340
2400
4900

3.

Out
4320
1940
3000
5500

4.

Out
3700
1320
2380
4880

5–8. Answers will vary.

PPM 124
Function machines

1.

Out	Out
5	20
6	18
8	40
7	70
8	16
8	48
4	36
6	42
13	52
12	72
19	171
82	656
85	85

2. − 20
3. Answers will vary.

PPM 125
Function machines

1.

In	Function	Out
32	÷ 4	8
27	÷ 3	9
40	÷ 5	8
36	÷ 6	6
42	÷ 7	6
64	÷ 8	8
45	÷ 8	5
60	÷ 4	15
81	÷ 3	27
130	÷ 10	13
96	÷ 2	48
154	÷ 7	22
136	÷ 8	17

2. × 6
3. Answers will vary.

PPM 126
Balancing

1. 60 + 60 = 120
2. 120 = 50 + 70
3. 100 + 20 = 40 + 80
4. $\frac{1}{2}$ of 260 = 100 + 30
5. 1630 − 1500 = 130
6. 130 = 75 + 55
7. 1000 = $\frac{1}{2}$ of 2000
8. $\frac{1}{4}$ of 4000 = 1000
9. 500 + 0 = $\frac{1}{2}$ of 1000
10–20. Answers will vary.

PPM 127
Make it balance!

1. $\frac{1}{2}$ of 64 — 32
   $\frac{1}{4}$ of 140 — 35
   $\frac{1}{10}$ of 350
   $\frac{1}{5}$ of 160
2. $\frac{1}{10}$ of 600 — 42
   $\frac{1}{5}$ of 300 — 60
   $\frac{1}{2}$ of 84
   $\frac{1}{4}$ of 168
3. $\frac{2}{3}$ of 60 — 40
   $\frac{1}{3}$ of 90 — 30
   $\frac{2}{3}$ of 45
   $\frac{1}{3}$ of 120
4. $\frac{1}{2}$ of 68 — 36
   $\frac{1}{2}$ of 72 — 34
   $\frac{2}{3}$ of 54
   $\frac{1}{3}$ of 102
5. $\frac{2}{3}$ of 75 — 25
   $\frac{1}{3}$ of 150 — 50
   $\frac{5}{5}$ of 25
   $\frac{1}{2}$ of 100
6. $\frac{1}{2}$ of 130 — 65
   $\frac{1}{2}$ of 132 — 66
   $\frac{2}{3}$ of 99
   $\frac{1}{4}$ of 264

7–8. Answers will vary.

PPM 128
Letters representing numbers

1. $n = 9$
2. $n = 8$
3. $n = 21$
4. $n = 12$
5. $n = 12$
6. $n = 12$
7. $n = 12$
8. $n = 11$
9. $n = 18$
10. $n = 32$
11. $n = 27$
12. $n = 38$
13. $n = 40$
14. $n = 7$
15. $n = 14$
16. $n = 22$
17. $n = 24$
18. $n = 54$
19. $n = 9$
20. $n = 7$
21. $n = 5$
22. Answers will vary.

PPM 129
Triangular patterns

1. 3, 6, 10, 15, 21, 28, 36, 45
2. 55
3. These are triangular numbers.

PPM 130
Pascal's triangle

1. Multiples of 3

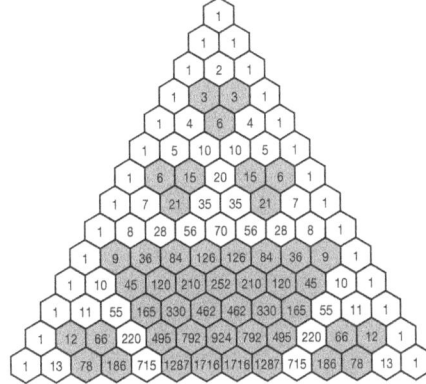

2. Multiples of 5

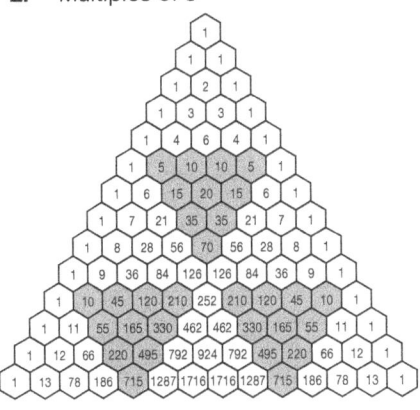

3. Multiples of 7

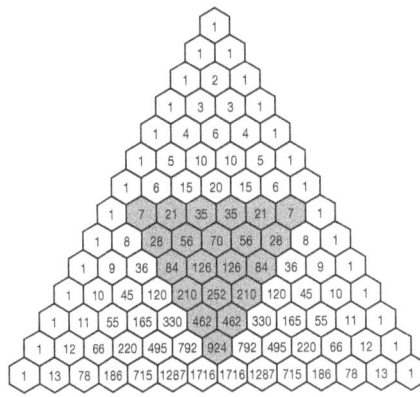

4. Odd numbers

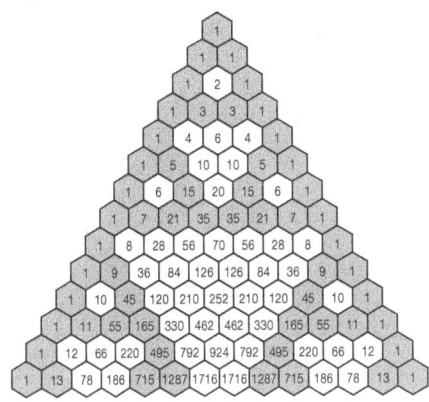

PPM 131
Function machine inputs

1.
In	Out
4	32
6	48
70	560
90	720
8	64
10	80

In	Out
5	35
3	21
6	42
100	700
9	63
8	56

Algebraic Thinking PPMs

In	Out
7	49
5	25
6	36
9	81
4	16
8	64

3.
In	Step 1	Step 2 and out
3	18	22
10	60	64
9	54	58
1	6	10
15	90	94
11	66	70

PPM 132
Two-step function machines

1.
In	Step 1	Step 2 and out
2	4	7
3	6	9
8	16	19
12	24	27

2.
In	Step 1	Step 2 and out
5	20	26
9	36	42
12	48	54
23	92	98

3.
In	Step 1	Step 2 and out
25	150	142
37	222	214
45	270	262
63	378	370

4.
In	Step 1	Step 2 and out
67	670	664
89	890	884
78	780	774
94	940	934

PPM 133
Triangular and square numbers

1.
Position	Triangular number	Made by adding
1st	1	1
2nd	3	1 + 2
3rd	6	1 + 2 + 3
4th	10	1 + 2 + 3 + 4
5th	15	1 + 2 + 3 + 4 + 5
6th	21	1 + 2 + 3 + 4 + 5 + 6
7th	28	1 + 2 + 3 + 4 + 5 + 6 + 7
8th	36	1 + 2 + 3 + 4 + 5 + 6 + 7 + 8
9th	45	1 + 2 + 3 + 4 + 5 + 6 + 7 + 8 + 9
10th	55	1 + 2 + 3 + 4 + 5 + 6 + 7 + 8 + 9 + 10

2.
Position	Square number	Made by adding	Made by adding triangular Nos	Positions of triangular nos
1st	1	1 × 1	1	1st
2nd	4	2 × 2	1 + 3	2nd
3rd	9	3 × 3	3 + 6	3rd
4th	16	4 × 4	6 + 10	4th
5th	25	5 × 5	10 + 15	5th
6th	36	6 × 6	15 + 21	6th
7th	49	7 × 7	21 + 28	7th
8th	64	8 × 8	28 + 36	8th
9th	81	9 × 9	36 + 45	9th
10th	100	10 × 10	44 + 55	10th

PPM 134
Which are which?

1. 27, 64, 125, 216; 343; cube number patterns.
   10, 15, 21, 28; 36; triangular number patterns.
   10, 9, 7·9, 6·7; 5·4; patterns with different sized steps.
   4, 6, 10, 16; 26; Fibonacci sequence.
   27, 26, 30, 29; 33; alternating pattern.
   100, 81, 64, 49; 36; square number pattern.

   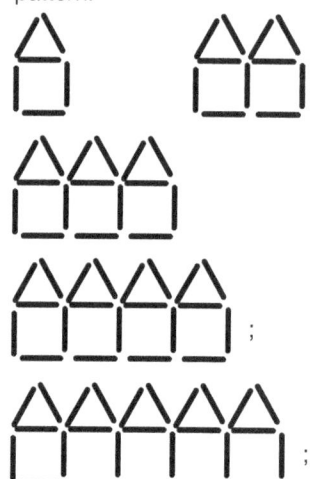
   visual pattern.
   4·2, 5·3, 6·4, 7·5; 8·6; patterns with equal sized steps.

2. Answers will vary

PPM 135
Reversing changes

1. Children's drawings should show a two-step function machine showing that:
   6 × 7 = 42 and then 42 + 4 = 48.
   They should then show the inverse of this function machine to check their answers:
   48 − 4 = 42 and then 42 ÷ 7 = 6.

2. Children's drawings should show a two-step function machine showing that:
   3 × 10 = 30 and then 30 ÷ 2 = 15.
   They should then show the inverse of this function machine to check their answers:
   15 × 2 = 30 and then 30 ÷ 10 = 3.

3. Children's drawings should show a two-step function machine showing that:
   7 × 6 = 42 and then 42 − 3 = 39.
   They should then show the inverse of this function machine to check their answers:
   39 + 3 = 42 and then 42 ÷ 6 = 7.

4. Children's drawings should show a two-step function machine showing that:
   210 ÷ 10 = 21 and then 21 + 7 = 28.
   They should then show the inverse

of this function machine to check their answers:
28 − 7 = 21 and then 21 × 10 = 210.

5. Children's drawings should show a two-step function machine showing that:
$45 ÷ 5 = 9$ and then $9 − 2 = 7$.
They should then show the inverse of this function machine to check their answers:
$7 + 2 = 9$ and then $9 × 5 = 45$.

6. Children's drawings should show a two-step function machine showing that:
$5 × 7 = 35$, $35 + 4 = 39$ and then $39 × 6 = 234$.
They should then show the inverse of this function machine to check their answers:
$234 ÷ 6 = 39$, $39 − 4 = 35$ and then $35 ÷ 7 = 5$.

7. Children's drawings should show a two-step function machine showing that:
$16 ÷ 4 = 4$ and then $4 + 5 = 9$.
They should then show the inverse of this function machine to check their answers:
$9 − 5 = 4$ and then $4 × 4 = 16$.

8. Children's drawings should show a two-step function machine showing that:
$4 × 7 = 28$, $28 + 4 = 32$ and then $32 + 4 = 36$.
They should then show the inverse of this function machine to check their answers:
$36 − 4 = 32$, $32 − 4 = 28$ and then $28 ÷ 7 = 4$.

PPM 136
More function machines

1. Children's drawings should show a two-step function machine showing that:
$n × 4 = 4n$ and then $4n + 6 = 22$.
They should then show the inverse of this function machine to find the solution:
$22 − 6 = 16$ and then $16 ÷ 4 = 4$ and therefore $n = 4$.

2. Children's drawings should show a two-step function machine showing that:
$n × 5 = 5n$ and then $5n + 4 = 39$.
They should then show the inverse of this function machine to find the solution:
$39 − 4 = 35$ and then $35 ÷ 5 = 7$ and therefore $n = 7$.

3. Children's drawings should show a two-step function machine showing that:
$n × 7 = 7n$ and then $7n + 8 = 29$.

They should then show the inverse of this function machine to find the solution:
$29 − 8 = 21$ and then $21 ÷ 7 = 3$ and therefore $n = 3$.

4. Children's drawings should show a two-step function machine showing that:
$n × 10 = 10n$ and then $10n + 7 = 47$.
They should then show the inverse of this function machine to find the solution:
$47 − 7 = 40$ and then $40 ÷ 10 = 4$ and therefore $n = 4$.

5. Answers will vary.

PPM 137
Solving equations

1. Children's drawings should show a two-step function machine showing that:
$x × 5 = 5x$ and then $5x − 6 = 24$.
They should then show the inverse of this function machine to find the solution:
$24 + 6 = 30$ and then $30 ÷ 5 = 6$ and therefore $x = 6$.

2. Children's drawings should show a two-step function machine showing that:
$x × 3 = 3x$ and then $3x − 4 = 11$.
They should then show the inverse of this function machine to find the solution:
$11 + 4 = 15$ and then $15 ÷ 3 = 5$ and therefore $x = 5$.

3. Children's drawings should show a two-step function machine showing that:
$x × 6 = 6x$ and then $6x + 2 = 26$.
They should then show the inverse of this function machine to find the solution:
$26 − 2 = 24$ and then $24 ÷ 6 = 4$ and therefore $x = 4$.

4. Children's drawings should show a two-step function machine showing that:
$x × 4 = 4x$ and then $4x + 6 = 34$.
They should then show the inverse of this function machine to find the solution:
$34 − 6 = 28$ and then $28 ÷ 4 = 7$ and therefore $x = 7$.

5. Children's drawings should show a two-step function machine showing that:
$x × 5 = 5x$ and then $5x + 7 = 42$.
They should then show the inverse of this function machine to find the solution:
$42 − 7 = 35$ and then $35 ÷ 5 = 7$ and therefore $x = 7$.

6. Children's drawings should show a two-step function machine showing that:
$x × 8 = 8x$ and then $8x − 7 = 41$.
They should then show the inverse of this function machine to find the solution:
$41 + 7 = 34$ and then $34 ÷ 8 = 4·25$ and therefore $x = 4·25$.

PPM 138
Solving equations using a function machine

1. Children's drawings should show a two-step function machine showing that:
$x + 3 = (x + 3)$ and then $(x + 3) × 5 = 30$.
They should then show the inverse of this function machine to find the solution:
$30 ÷ 5 = 6$ and then $6 − 3 = 3$ and therefore $x = 3$.

2. Children's drawings should show a two-step function machine showing that:
$x + 9 = (x + 9)$ and then $(x + 9) × \frac{1}{2} = 10$.
They should then show the inverse of this function machine to find the solution:
$10 ÷ \frac{1}{2} = 20$ and then $20 − 9 = 11$ and therefore $x = 11$.

3. Children's drawings should show a two-step function machine showing that:
$x − 7 = (x − 7)$ and then $(x − 7) × 6 = 18$.
They should then show the inverse of this function machine to find the solution:
$18 ÷ 6 = 3$ and then $3 + 7 = 10$ and therefore $x = 10$.

4. Children's drawings should show a two-step function machine showing that:
$x + 6 = (x + 6)$ and then $(x + 6) × 4 = 28$.
They should then show the inverse of this function machine to find the solution:
$28 ÷ 4 = 7$ and then $7 − 6 = 1$ and therefore $x = 1$.

5. Children's drawings should show a two-step function machine showing that:
$x − 3 = (x − 3)$ and then $(x − 3) × \frac{1}{4} = 2$.
They should then show the inverse of this function machine to find the solution:
$2 ÷ \frac{1}{4} = 8$ and then $8 + 3 = 11$ and therefore $x = 11$.

Algebraic Thinking PPMs

6. Children's drawings should show a two-step function machine showing that:
$x - \frac{1}{2} = (x - \frac{1}{2})$ and then $(x - \frac{1}{2}) \times \frac{1}{10} = \frac{1}{2}$.
They should then show the inverse of this function machine to find the solution:
$\frac{1}{2} \div \frac{1}{10} = 5$ and then $5 + \frac{1}{2} = 5\cdot5$ and therefore $x = 5\cdot5$.

7. Answers will vary.

PPM 139
Solving equations

1. $x + 4 = 12$
   $x + 4 - 4 = 12 - 4$
   $x = 12 - 4$
   $x = 8$
2. $x = 8$
3. $x = 6$
4. $x = 11$
5. $x = 8$
6. $x = 12$
7. $x = 4$
8. $x = 3$
9. $x = 9$
10. Answers will vary.

PPM 140
Solving equations

1. $x + 10 = 13$
   $x + 10 - 10 = 13 - 10$
   $x = 13 - 10$
   $x = 3$
2. $x = 35$
3. $x = 60$
4. $x = 63$
5. $x = 21$
6. $x = 43$
7. $x = 14$
8. $x = 6\cdot6$
9. $x = 5\cdot4$
10. Answers will vary.

PPM 141
Solving equations using multiplication facts

1. $6n = 42$
   $6n \div 6 = 42 \div 6$
   $n = 42 \div 6$
   $n = 7$
2. $n = 10$
3. $n = 11$
4. $n = 8$
5. $n = 5$
6. $n = 9$
7. $n = 20$
8. $n = 48$
9. $n = 30$
10. Answers will vary.

Algebraic Thinking APMs

APM 453
Move that table!

1. The 8 times-table. It has been shifted back by 1.
2. The 3 times-table. It has been shifted forward by 6.
3. The 20 times-table. It has been shifted back by 13.
4. The 9 times-table. It has been shifted forward by 4.
5. The 50 times-table. It has been shifted forward by 16.
6. The 12 times-table. It has been shifted back by 4.

The method is to find the difference between the numbers in the sequence to find the times-table. Then find the difference between the times-table number and the first number in the sequence to find the shift.

7. The 15 times-table. It has been shifted forward by 6.
8. The 100 times-table. It has been shifted forward by 34.

If the numbers are all odd or even then it is an even number times-table. If the numbers are both odd and even then it is an odd number times-table.
If the units digit is always the same it is the times-table of a multiple of 10. If there are two different units digits it is the times-table of a multiple of 5.

APM 455
More pyramids

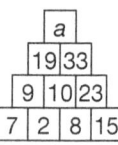

$a = 19 + 33 = 52$

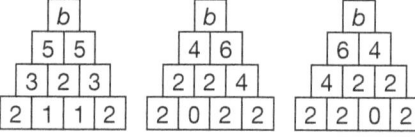

$b = 5 + 5 = 10$ or $b = 4 + 6 = 10$
Answers will vary but should include any from $x = 24, y = 1$; $x = 21, y = 2$; $x = 18, y = 3$; $x = 15, y = 4$; $x = 12, y = 5$; $x = 9, y = 6$; $x = 6, y = 7$; or $x = 3, y = 8$.
There are eight possible pairs of values. When the value of y increases by 1, the value of x decreases by 3.

APM 456
Shape puzzles

1. ● = 4
2. ● = 16
3. ● = 76
4. ● = 16
5. ● = 0
6. ● = 19·5

APM 457
Pattern puzzle

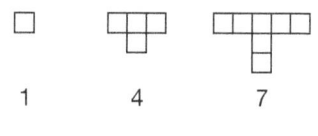

1   4   7

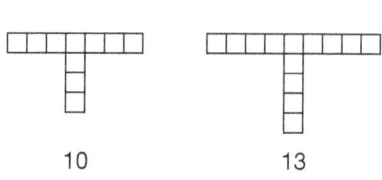

10   13

There will be 298 squares in the 100th term of this pattern.
You can use the formula $3n - 2$ to work this out.

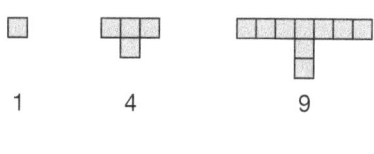

1   4   9

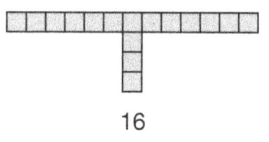

16

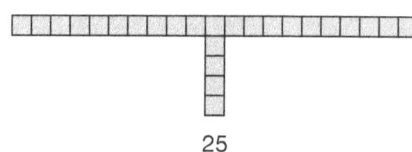

25

There will be 10 000 squares in the 100th term of this pattern.
You can use the formula n^2 to work this out.

APM 458
Dots and squares

24 lines, 25 dots

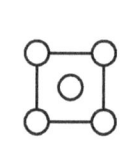 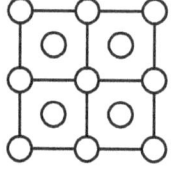

4 lines, 5 dots   12 lines, 13 dots

25 units long:
1300 lines
1301 dots

100 units long:
20 200 lines
20 201 dots

lines = $2((n + 1)n)$ or $(n^2 + (n + 1)^2) - 1$
dots = $n^2 + (n + 1)^2$ or $2((n + 1)n) + 1$

APM 459
Fibonacci

1. 1 1 2 3 <u>5</u> <u>8</u> <u>13</u> <u>21</u> <u>34</u> <u>55</u>
2. ⁻21 13 ⁻8 5 ⁻3 2 ⁻1 1 0 1

Children should notice that this reflects the first sequence, but alternating between positive and negative numbers.

3. $1 \div 1 = 1$
4. $2 \div 1 = 2$
5. $3 \div 2 = 1\cdot5$
6. $5 \div 8 = 1\cdot6666\ldots$
   $8 \div 5 = 1\cdot6$
   $13 \div 8 = 1\cdot625$
   $21 \div 13 = 1\cdot615384\ldots$
   $34 \div 21 = 1\cdot619047\ldots$
   $55 \div 34 = 1\cdot617647\ldots$

Children should notice that all the answers are 1·6 to the nearest 1 decimal place.

7. Answers will vary.
8. Answers will vary.
9. Answers will vary.
10. Answers will vary.
11. Children should notice that all the answers to the numbers generated in their sequence are still 1·6 to the nearest 1 decimal place.
12. Two numbers are in the Golden ratio if the ratio of the larger number to the sum of the two numbers is equal to the ratio of the larger number to the smaller number. The Golden ratio is approximately 1·6180339887 which is 1·6 to the nearest 1 decimal place, just like the answers found by dividing the numbers in the Fibonacci sequence.

APM 460
Function machines

Children should notice that the crosses on the graph, when joined, form a straight line.

APM 461
Letter values

A = 8   B = 24   C = 26   D = 8
E = 4   F = 8   G = 20

APM 463
Consecutive numbers

Children should notice that the formula for 3 consecutive numbers is *3M*, the formula for 5 consecutive numbers is *5M* and the formula for 7 consecutive number is *7M*.

Part of Pearson

Heinemann is an imprint of Pearson Education Limited, a company incorporated in England and Wales, having its registered office at Edinburgh Gate, Harlow, Essex, CM20 2JE. Registered company number: 872828

www.pearsonschools.co.uk

Heinemann is a registered trademark of Pearson Education Limited

Text © Pearson Education Limited 2010

First published 2010

18
10

British Library Cataloguing in Publication Data
A catalogue record for this book is available from the British Library

ISBN 978 0 435 04334 6

Copyright notice
All rights reserved. No part of this publication may be reproduced in any form or by any means (including photocopying or storing it in any medium by electronic means and whether or not transiently or incidentally to some other use of this publication) without the written permission of the copyright owner, except in accordance with the provisions of the Copyright, Designs and Patents Act 1988 or under the terms of a licence issued by the Copyright Licensing Agency, Saffron House, 6–10 Kirby Street, London EC1N 8TS (www.cla.co.uk). Applications for the copyright owner's written permission should be addressed to the publisher.

Typeset by Tech-Set Ltd, Gateshead
Cover design by Pearson Education Limited
Cover illustration by Volker Beisler © Pearson Education Limited
Printed in Great Britain by Ashford Colour Press Ltd

Acknowledgements
Every effort has been made to contact copyright holders of material reproduced in this book. Any omissions will be rectified in subsequent printings if notice is given to the publishers.